# WALKING

### 28 circular walks with maps and directions
### (and suggestions for many more...)

### Walked, written and photographed by
# Judy Smith

a RED DOG guide book

Previously published as 'Holiday Walks in Brittany'
by Sigma Press, 2001
This revised and extensively re-worked edition is
published as 'Walking Brittany' by Red Dog Books, 2005
ISBN 0 9536001 4 9

**For our grandson Jacob
We hope that you too
will enjoy the wild landscape
of Brittany one day**

Main cover picture - misty morning on Lac de Guerlédan

The right of Judy Smith to be identified as the author of this
work is asserted in accordance with sections 77 and 78 of the
Copyright Designs and Patents Act 1988

British Library Cataloguing-in-Publication Data
A catalogue record for this book is available from the British Library

Red Dog Books is based in Axbridge, Somerset and in Brittany.
Enquiries should be addressed to the editorial office at
Red Dog Books, 29410 Plounéour-Ménez, France.

email: reddogbooks@tiscali.fr

www.reddogbooks.com

Printed and bound in China

# Contents

## WALKS 1 to 6 - Ille-et-Vilaine

## WALKS 7 to 8 - Loire-Atlantique

## WALKS 9 to 11 - Morbihan

## WALKS 12 to 19 - Côtes d'Armor

## WALKS 20 to 28 - Finistère

**Cancale**

# INTRODUCING THE FOOTPATHS OF BRITTANY

Brittany brings to mind many images - cliffs and seascapes, fishing villages and forests, folk-lore and festivals, religion, legend and pre-history. It is a land almost separate from the rest of France, temperamentally as well as geographically; a land jutting far into the Atlantic Ocean, a land with many miles of coastline. The unspoilt and beautiful beaches are well-known to British holiday-makers. Very much less well-known is that Brittany has more waymarked paths than any other region of France and that Tourist Offices are often stocked with a good supply of maps and routes. Add to this the mild climate of Brittany - in winter, temperatures are close to those on the Cote d'Azur - and you can see that it is the ideal destination for a vacation on foot. But whether you are considering a full walking holiday in Brittany, or just want to escape from the beach for a few hours, this book should have something to offer you.

Bretons are no strangers to long-distance walking. Until a few hundred years ago, every Breton, at least once in his lifetime, was expected to undertake a walk of over 400 miles, to be completed in under a month. The walk was the famous Tro Breiz, a pilgrimage visiting each of the seven cathedrals of Brittany - Quimper, St-Pol-de-Léon, Tréguier, Saint-Brieuc, Saint-Malo, Dol-de-Bretagne and Vannes. If the walk was not taken in life, the threat was that the Breton soul must take it after death, advancing along the route by one coffin length every seven years! No such heroics are demanded by the walks in this book: they are all simple circular routes between 3 and 10 miles in length, and many have short cuts as well, which means that most of them are suitable for all the family. But before you set out, here are just a few words about what you will find on foot in Brittany.

The ancient Celts perceived Brittany to be in two parts - Armor, the coast, and Argoat, the forested inland country. This simple division is apparent today. The coast is the destination of most holidaymakers - and, of course, it is simply splendid! One of the most scenic footpaths in Europe, the GR 34, runs along almost the whole length of this shoreline. You could get off the boat at St-Malo and follow it west to Roscoff, pick it up again on the west coast, and follow it south around Cornouaille almost to the Gulf of Morbihan - a distance of over 600 miles. If that seems a little far for a holiday, the circular walks in this book include some of the best stretches - the famous Sentier des Douaniers on the Pink

Granite Coast, the beautiful Cap d'Erquy, the cliffs of the Crozon peninsula, the rocky Pointe du Grouin in the north and the wild Pointe du Raz in the west, the estuaries of the Rance and of the Trieux and lots more.

The Argoat, inland Brittany, may be something of a surprise if you have not explored it before. Brittany's spine is two ranges of hills, the Monts d'Arrée and the Montagnes Noires, hills that are older than almost any in the world. Worn down over 600 million years, the summits are now rounded humps of granite and schist, broken in places by jagged outcrops of quartz. These hills are covered in wild moorland and dense forest, and cut through by deep gorges where rivers cascade in dramatic fashion, often disappearing beneath a 'chaos' of rounded boulders long since split from the granite. Walking here is on the wild side! Climb along the ridge top above the Gorges du Daoulas, trek across the moors to the lonely chapel on the high summit of Ménez-Mikel, or follow the little stream that bounces its way through the Gorges du Corong and then vanishes under the rock. A walk not to be missed is that at Huelgoat, where cascades, chasms, pools and strange rock formations are found deep in the ancient forest. Seeking more gentle scenery, you could try a ramble through the beech woods of Fougères or le Faouët, follow the winding river Aven or stroll beside the locks of the Ille-et-Rance Canal.

But Brittany offers more than fine landscapes. This is a land where prehistoric man left more evidence of his occupation than almost anywhere else in Europe. Many of the routes in this book pass by a megalith or an ancient burial chamber of some kind, often in a remote place, accessible only on foot. Walking in the region of the Abers, you will find some of the tallest standing stones in all France. Far away in the east of Brittany, a walk across the moors brings you to the most amazing collection of megaliths at St-Just.

Above everything else, Brittany is a celtic land - a land that has much in common with Cornwall and Wales and Ireland, a land reviving its ancient language (I have included a few relevant words at the back of this book), an enchanted land full of mythology, legend and superstition. Almost every walk has a story attached to some part of it. The Devil makes his presence known all over the place - every cave is a 'Grotte du Diable' and every standing stone is a petrified sinner or was dropped by fairies on their way to build Mont.St-Michel. The legend of the ill-fated lovers Tristan and Isolde has cast its spell on the west coast, and the Bay of

Douarnenez is home to the story of the lost city of Ys, Brittany's answer to Atlantis. The Breton troubadours of the Middle Ages set the stories of King Arthur and the Knights of the Round Table in the forest of Paimpont - it became the Brocéliande of the legend. You can walk in the woods to find the Château de Comper, the home of the Lady of the Lake, seek out Merlin's seat on the edge of the Valley of no Return, visit the Fountain of Barenton where Merlin first met the Fairy Viviane - and sample the waters of the Fountain of Youth which he drank to keep at bay the signs of his advancing years.

There are so many fine walks in Brittany that choosing among them has proved extremely difficult. If you think of each route in this book as a taste of walking in that area, you can explore the 'More walks' section to find your own favourites. The friendly tourist offices should be able to provide you with further information - and if you are worried about French texts, the 'Useful French Walking Words' on page 159 might shed some light. Tourist offices can also be very helpful if you explain that you need a bus or a taxi  to drop you at some point 10 miles down the line to enjoy a quiet walk home along a Grande Randonnée. With each walk I have included just a few suggestions of places of interest in the area - often associated with the walk, or with special appeal to walkers.

I have enjoyed exploring again the paths of Brittany for this book. Special thanks are due to Eric, my husband, who walked every one of the routes with me (sometimes more than once) and was (reasonably!) patient with my desire to visit every walk mentioned in the More walks section as well. In one year we must have covered more than 800 miles on foot! I am also grateful to the friends and acquaintances who have helped with all manner of enquiries. My thanks go too to the 'Offices du Tourisme' of Brittany - they were more than generous with time and information and I am sure that they will help you in the same way.

I hope you will enjoy this very different journey through Brittany. It only remains to wish you Chañs vat deoc'h - and you can work that one out for yourselves!

# Maps

The outline maps provided with each walk in this book show all the major junctions and orientations necessary for following the route in conjunction with the full written directions. If you want to explore a particular area in more detail, reference numbers for the large scale (1:25,000) IGN Série Bleue maps are given in the notes at the beginning of each walk.

**All directions in this book reflect the situation at the time of writing. Please note that paths and waymarked circuits *may* change in response to local conditions.**

# Map Symbols

| | | | |
|---|---|---|---|
| ✧ | archaeological or historical feature | † | calvary or wayside cross |
| ✳ | belvedere/viewpoint | ☆ | fort |
| ⌇ | bridge | ☖ | fontaine/spring |
| ▬ | building(s) | ◌ | menhir (standing stone) |
| ⋏ | campsite | ⊓ | dolmen (burial chamber) |
| + | chapel | P | parking |
| ⊹ | château (fort) | ▲ | peak |
| ⚲ | church or chapel | ① | reference point in the directions |

# Abbreviations

GR = Grande Randonnée - long distance footpath
GRP = Grande Randonée du Pays - regional footpath
PR = Promenade et Randonnée - local circular walk
km(s) = kilometres (1 kilometre = 5/8 mile)
TO = tourist office
VTT = Vélo Tout Terrain (mountain bike)

**Other useful terms**
Parcours Sportif - sport/fitness trail
Sentier Côtier - coastal path

# A LITTLE HISTORY TO SET THE SCENE

## The Megalithic Period

The multitude of megaliths are obvious signs of Brittany's early occupation, but little is known of the people who built them. Most are dated between 5000 and 2000 BC - the dolmens and gallery graves are generally the earliest, while the menhirs, standing alone or in alignments, tend to date from around the end of this period. The east-west orientation of many alignments and the discovery of primitive 'calendars' (see Walk 4) suggest that these people were sun-worshippers and early farmers who needed to predict the seasons. The latest megaliths (from the Bronze Age) have yielded grave-goods such as jewellery, decorated pottery and other artefacts now to be found in the museums at Vannes and Rennes.

## Celts and Romans

Around 600 BC the first wave of Celts arrived in Brittany, which they called Armor, the Land of the Sea. Warlike and tribal, they were also farmers, finally subjugated by the Romans after their most prominent tribe the Veneti lost an epic sea battle in 56 BC. The Romans brought civilisation, but little remains of their occupation (although you can see the vestiges of a Roman aqueduct on a walk near Maël-Carhaix). Armor became the Roman Armorica.

In the fifth century AD, the Roman legions were recalled to fight battles nearer home, leaving France vulnerable to invaders. Tribes of Angles and Saxons also pushed Britain's population to the south-west, and from there across the sea to Armorica. From Ireland, Wales and Cornwall came the second wave of Celts: they called their new country Brittany (little Britain). These Celts were a Christian people. They soon converted their adopted land, providing the country with its abundance of saints.

## The Duchy of Brittany

In 799, Brittany was seized by Charlemagne, whose son Louis gave a Breton, Nominoë, the title 'Duke of Brittany'. Nominoë's son, Erispoë, went one step farther and called himself king, but Brittany was a kingdom for a mere hundred years. After the death of King Alain Barbe-Torte in 952, there followed around 400 years of trouble and disorder, culminating in the War of the Succession. In 1364, the Montforts (supported by England) emerged victorious, restored order to Brittany and ensured its prosperity for the next hundred years. The famous Breton warrior du Guesclin fought on the French side in this war and eventually became Constable of France.

9

Throughout this time, Brittany was a Duchy independent of France. In 1483, the redoubtable Anne of Brittany became duchess and later married Charles VIII, King of France. When he died in an accident, she went on to marry his brother, Louis XII, but still retained independence for Brittany. After her death, the Duchy passed to her daughter Claude, who, after her marriage to the future François I, relinquished her birthright. In 1532, the union of Brittany and France was ratified at the Parliament of Vannes.

## French Brittany

Brittany was given a French governor and a parliamentary assembly in Nantes. This was an affluent period when many elaborate châteaux sprang up and religious building and art flourished (see Parish Closes, pages 115 & 136). In 1610 Louis XIII acceded to the throne and began stripping the vast forests of the interior to build warships. In the reign of Louis XIV, heavy taxes were demanded to fund his extravagant tastes and the people began to rebel. The famous 'Stamped Paper Revolt' of 1675 (against tax on all paper used for legal documents) was squashed with much bloodshed. Pewter and tobacco were taxed and an army of peasants calling themselves the Bonnets Rouges (Redcaps) rampaged through Brittany. The rebellion was again crushed with excessive brutality. From this period came Vauban, soldier, military architect and, at first, a friend of Louis XIV. His fortifications are seen all around the coasts of Brittany, for example at Carantec and Camaret, Perros-Guirec and Cap Fréhel, among others. He too became disillusioned with the Royalists and fell from favour before he died in 1707.

## The French Revolution

Brittany continued to resent its French domination, and in the 18th century, initially supported the Revolutionaries against the king and aristocracy. But soon it became apparent that the new regime brought yet more problems for Brittany. The Revolutionaries made laws against the Priests, threatened the Breton language and demanded conscription to the army of a country to which the Bretons felt no allegiance. The despotic governor Carrier drowned thousands of supposed Royalists in the Loire. So arose the Association Bretonne - the anti-Revolutionary movement popularly known as the Chouans. Their name derived from *chat huant*, the cry of the screech owl, which they used as a night-time signal. The last Chouan was executed in 1804 but the Bretons still tell stories of their exploits and there are many markers and memorials. After the Reign of Terror, Napoleon and his victories brought some peace and pride to France - and to Brittany too - and the final Breton revolt was squashed in 1832.

## More recent history

The 19th century saw the decline of Brittany's fishing industry and the conversion of much wild moorland to agriculture. Brittany began to re-assert its unique identity and folklore. Two great Breton writers of this time were Châteaubriand and Jules Verne. Artists flocked to experience the wildness of Brittany, among them Gauguin and his school of synthetists who lodged at Pont-Aven in the 1880s.

The early 20th century brought the Great War in which Brittany suffered greatly. Being a seafaring people, its men joined the Navy, and Brittany lost a larger part of its population than any other region of France. In World War II its role was glorious - Bretons eagerly responded to de Gaulle's cry to join the Free French army, and indeed, a quarter of that force were Breton. The Breton Resistance was active and operated many escape routes across the Channel. The main ports of Brittany, Brest, St-Nazaire, Lorient and St-Malo were all destroyed.

Soon after the war's end, a new committee was formed to safeguard the interests of Brittany - the Comité d'Études et de Liaisons des Intérêts Bretons. This was a turning point for the economy of Brittany and for her nationalism. The Breton flag had been designed by Morvan Marchal back in 1926. Called the Gwenn ha du (white and black), it is the only flag not to use colour. It can be seen flying all over Brittany from public buildings to boats in the harbours. In schools the language is again promoted and it is estimated that more than 250,000 people speak Breton. Traditional folk music is heard in the many festivals. Since 1985, bi-lingual road signs have been introduced.

Brittany's tourist industry has grown steadily since the last war. The coastline is still almost entirely unspoiled, and completely lacking the more garish trappings of commercialism that have invaded many British resorts. The beaches are perfect for a family holiday, and both coast and inland are gaining a reputation for walking. Nearly a million Britons now visit Brittany every year, making it one of our most popular holiday destinations.

**Dolmen de Guilligui**

11

# WALKING IN FRANCE

France is almost certainly the best country for walking in Europe. The excellence of the footpaths is due almost entirely to an organisation called the Féderation Française de la Randonnée Pédestre - The FFRP - who over the last half century have waymarked and described routes of all kinds throughout France. Many of the walks in this book are based on their routes. Their long distance paths, the Grandes Randonnées (GR), are the best waymarked paths imaginable, and will invariably lead you past all the most interesting features and best viewpoints in an area. Next there are the Grandes Randonnées du Pays (GRP), round tours of an area or region which may take, in walking time, anything from a couple of days to a week. They aim to show you the best a region has to offer. And finally there are the Promenades et Randonnées (PR), the equivalent of our shorter circular walks, sprinkled generously over the whole country.

Each of these route types has its own waymarks, painted on trees, rocks, telegraph poles, or any other convenient surface - the Grandes Randonnées are marked white on red, the Grandes Randonnées du Pays yellow on red and the Promenades et Randonnées, yellow. The signage warns of every turn before you reach it, and a cross indicates 'wrong way' if you have missed it. Nothing could be more simple! In fairness, it must be said that although Grandes Randonnées are invariably superbly waymarked, the state of a Promenade et Randonnée may reflect the level of enthusiasm of the local tourist board or walking group. Even so, most are very good.

Another excellent feature of walking in France is that most paths are open to you - only those marked 'Privé' deny you access. It is accepted that you will not wander on crops or gardens, leave litter or pick flowers. It should be mentioned that in winter some forest paths are temporarily closed for the period of the hunting season, generally from November to February, but these paths will again be marked. In France, farmers and landowners seem much more in tune with walkers than in England and will generally greet you cheerfully. If you can manage just a 'Bonjour' in return it is certain to go down well.

And now the footpaths of France await you - and they are guaranteed to be addictive. Take one short stretch of a Grande Randonnée and you may well be hooked for life!

# Ille-et-Vilaine

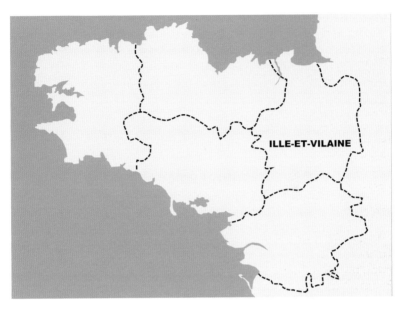

ILLE-ET-VILAINE

Château de Trécesson

## WALK 1 - In the Forest of FOUGÈRES

| Length 5kms | Time 1¼hrs | Level Easy |
| --- | --- | --- |

**Location & parking:** Ferme de Chênedet. Take the D177 north-east from Fougères, direction St-Hilaire-du-Harcouët. Once in the forest, turn left at the crossroads, signed Chênedet. At the farm and equestrian centre, the road bears right, and there are then several small parking areas on the left, before the T-junction. From these, the lake can be seen through the trees.

**Refreshments:** none in the forest but plenty in Fougères.

**Notes:** walking boots recommended - the forest can be muddy in winter or after wet weather. Swimming possible in summer from the sandy beach at the lake. An excellent *parcours sportif* (fitness course) encircles the lake. (Map: IGN Série Bleue 1317 E)

## Introduction

Fougères is known for its fine medieval castle – and for its splendid beech forest where history, legend and recreation all have their part. This short walk visits a prehistoric dolmen, a Roman hill fort and the site of an ancient healing tree before returning to the lake where you can picnic and swim.

'I would like to ask everyone, have you seen Fougères?' So wrote Victor Hugo after he visited the town that was to be the setting for one of his novels. It is easy to understand his enthusiasm – there cannot be a more magnificent castle anywhere. Its dark walls, turrets, watch towers, moat and drawbridge are the epitome of medieval military architecture. Seen floodlit on a winter's night, its thirteen conical towers rising eerily from the river mists, it is sure to send a shiver down even the most well-insulated spine.

Fougères itself was a sort of frontier town, on the border between Brittany and the rest of France. It was the town that saw the start of the Chouan movement, the resistance of the Royalists of Brittany to the French Revolutionaries. In truth the Bretons were not so much Royalists as resisting conscription to the French army. Balzac chose Fougères as the setting for his historical tale Les Chouans, and Victor Hugo's Quatre-Vingt-Treize likewise told of the uprising of 1793. Fougères is a town steeped in history.

To the north of the town lies a vast forest of beech and oak, and this also has its connections with the Chouans. At one forest entrance, a cross marks their first encounter with the Revolutionary forces. In the woods nearby you can see the steps and gateway to the cellars of Landéan, dating from the 12th century. They were built by Raoul II, Baron of Fougères, to conceal his possessions from the English under Henry II. More treasure was said to be hidden deep in the forest under the *Pierre du Trésor*. This huge stone unfortunately collapsed when someone clumsily decided to seek his fortune. The well

The cellars of Landéan

laid out forest trails visit these and other historical and legendary sites – a Roman camp, dolmens, a line of standing stones, the vestiges of a convent and some ancient fortifications are scattered in the undergrowth, while through the heart of the forest runs the old salt-smugglers road. In medieval times, salt was not taxed in Brittany, making its cost a mere twentieth of that over the border. This route through the forest was preferable to the main road for the smugglers, but, even so, it was the scene of many bloodthirsty encounters with customs officers.

The route chosen for this walk is a compound of several marked trails. Deep in the forest is a lake where bathing and canoeing are possible in summer. Starting from here, you follow a GR through beech and pine woods to reach a prehistoric site known as the *Dolmen de la Pierre Courcoulée* or the 'Huguenot Stone'. This huge dolmen, now broken in two and sunken into the ground, once stood high on twelve legs. Breton forests are always places of legend, and soon you pass a cross that marks the site of a long-gone much-venerated beech tree, the *Fouteau de Poulailler*. To ensure recovery from illness, peasants would dance around the tree, sweeping the ground with a holly branch, and place an egg between its roots. Pieces of bark taken from the tree helped with the cure. A little farther up the hill, the remains of a Roman hill fort can be found in the undergrowth. After passing a restored old mill, the way returns through the woodland, and you can look out for deer and wild boar – and the mischievous forest goblin.

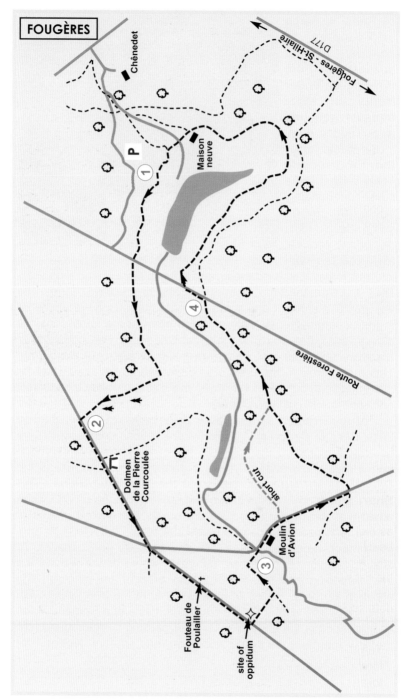

FOUGÈRES

Chênedet

Fougères - St-Hilaire D177

P

(1)

Maison neuve

(4)

Route Forestière

(2)

Π

Dolmen de la Pierre Courcoulée

short cut

Moulin d'Avion

(3)

Fouteau de Poulailler

site of oppidum

16

# Directions

1. From any of the parking spaces, walk through the trees towards the lake. You will cross a broad path which is the route of the GR – white on red flashes on the trees. Turn right on this path and follow it as it weaves through the woods, crossing directly over a stony track and then by a log bridge over a stream. Shortly afterwards, on reaching a plantation of conifers, the route turns sharp right. Five minutes walking through the conifers brings you to a wide stony track. Here turn left, and shortly, on the left, find the *Dolmen de la Pierre Courcoulée.*

2. Continue along the stony track to the cross-roads at its end – the Carrefour de Poulailler. Here cross the road and, now leaving the GR, bear left uphill, on the Route Forestière des Courbes. After about 200m, you reach the cross marking the site of the *Fouteau de Poulailler.* Continue up the hill, and, approaching the summit, look out for a long ridge mound in the undergrowth on the left. This is the wall of the hill-fort - turn left on a rather overgrown track going right through it. The track heads steeply downhill and soon meets a wide earthen track that is part of the VTT route (yellow flashes). Turn left on this track, which, after about 150m, bears right to come down to a road.

3. Turn right on this road, cross over the stream and pass the mill (Moulin d'Avion). The path you are now seeking is the orange-marked bridleway, which turns left from this road in about 250m.

---

**Short cut:** If the road seems too busy – or you fancy a forest adventure – take instead the first path on the left after the mill, just as the road corners right. This brings you into a rough field full of beech trees. In this field, keep straight ahead parallel to the wall on your left – you will see a yellow dot on a tree. When the wall ends, the track bears to the right. Continue on this rather vague track, and just as you begin to think you have got it all wrong, suddenly yellow dots appear all around you to lead you on to meet the bridleway, which is a rather narrow, but obvious, earthy track.

---

Turn left on the bridleway and follow the orange dots through the forest (not always easy as many of them are obscured by foliage). Eventually you emerge on a stony road.

**4**. Here turn left, and after about 60m on this road, turn right on a track that heads for the lake. After crossing a little stream, you meet the path that encircles the lake. The *parcours sportif* runs alongside, so if you are feeling that this short walk has not really given you enough exercise, you are now in a position to do something about it. Continue following this path to the right. At the far end of the lake it swings away through an attractive spinney before returning to the lakeside buildings. Here leave the track (the track ahead was part of the old salt-smugglers road) and keep beside the earthen wall behind the wooden buildings. After crossing the tarmac road, you again pick up the markings of the GR, and from there can return to your car.

## More walks in the area

- The TO in Fougères has information about all the various forest trails, which are very suitable for family walks, and also walking around the town itself (a 2km tour).
- The area around Antrain and the valley of the river Couesnon have several marked circuits through the woods and beside the river.
- The GR34 passes through the Forest of Fougères, and an attractive 12km hike to the north-west along it will take you to the old town of St-Germain-en-Coglès.

## Places of interest nearby

- The town of Fougères has a magnificent castle, the exquisite gothic church of St-Sulpice, medieval streets and many fine viewpoints.
- Legendary places include the Saut Roland in a valley at Dompierre to the south. Here a Prefect of the Marches of Brittany tried three times to jump the gap between huge rocks on his horse, falling to his death on the last attempt. An imprint of a horse-shoe marks the spot, and a nearby constant fall of water into a rocky basin is said to be the tears of his beloved, crying until judgement day.
- Near Noyal-sous-Bazouges is a huge stone known as le Pierre Longue. It was apparently dropped by the devil on his way to build St Michael's Mount. In fact it is a menhir, now topped by a cross in an attempt to christianise the pagan site.

## WALK 2 - Around the POINTE du GROUIN

| Length 6kms | Time 2hrs | Level Moderate |
|---|---|---|

**Location & parking:** the sea front at Port-Mer. From Cancale (14km east of St-Malo), head north towards Pointe du Grouin, turning right after 3kms (signed Port-Mer). There is parking along the sea front.

**Refreshments:** restaurant at the Pointe du Grouin, open in summer; various bar/restaurants along the sea-front at Port-Mer. More in Cancale.

**Notes:** this short walk is on good paths, quite suitable for trainers, but not really suitable for young children (paths are narrow and running along steep cliffs). Good distant views from the Point (where there are telescopes). Swimming beach at the Plage des Saussayes or at Port-Mer. (Map: IGN Top 25 1116 ET or Top 25 1215 OT)

## Introduction

East of St-Malo, the rocky finger of the Pointe du Grouin guards the entrance to the bay of Mont.St-Michel. A coastal path winds around the cliffs to reach its rugged tip, where there are fine views of the coastline from Cotentin to Cap Fréhel.

There is an old saying that the tide comes in across St-Michael's Bay faster than a horse can gallop. Perhaps it was originally meant as a warning to wandering equestrians, but at any rate it creates a dramatic picture of what happens here. At high tide, there is a bay of sparkling blue water; at low tide there are grey mudflats as far as the eye can see, broken only by the posts where mussels are cultivated and the dark rectangular oyster beds. The region for mussel farming is in the south of the bay near le-Vivier-sur-Mer, while Cancale, just below the Pointe du Grouin is the centre for oysters – although the young ones, the spats, are actually imported from near Auray in the Gulf of Morbihan and only 'grown on' here.

Cancale is a fascinating place. Below the main town is the port area where you can watch the comings and goings of the oyster farmers at low tide and survey the plethora of stalls laden with gnarled crustaceans. The air smells of salt and iodine and fish, and chippings of more shells scrunch beneath your feet. Oysters, it seems, are not simply oysters - there are bélons and creuses and pieds de cheval, the latter being huge and very expensive. If you are not a do-it-yourself oyster-eater, the town sports a mere fifty or so restaurants that will serve you with the delicacy – although surprisingly the prices here are often as high as you might find in Paris!

**Pointe du Grouin**

There is a good coastal path all the way from Cancale to the Pointe du Grouin, but in order to provide a circular walk, this route starts from Port-Mer, a very pretty little village up the coast. Port-Mer has no port, but boasts a fine sandy bay between rocky headlands and, of course, a few restaurants serving oysters. The path from here is a GR that hugs the cliff-face all the way, with views across the bay. Before you reach the Point, there is a restaurant and parking area - with the result that, at least in summer, you are unlikely to have the place to yourself. Farther along comes a signalling station, and then the Point itself, a long, rocky promontory of wild moorland, some 40m above the sea. Beside it is the Île des Landes, a long bare outcrop, now a bird sanctuary, and beyond this, a lighthouse clings to yet another rock. On a clear day, the views are superb and there is a toposcope to help you pick out the various features. Out to sea are the Îles Chaussey, farther over is Granville on the Normandy coast, and behind across the bay, the well-known outline of Mont.St-Michel can be seen.

On the west side of the Point is the Brittany coast, sweeping in rocky curves past St-Malo to Cap Fréhel. On this side, the path is at times even more precarious as it threads its way along steep slopes of gorse and bracken high above the sea. Arriving at civilisation in the form of another sandy beach, it is time to return to Port-Mer. This short but exhilarating walk should leave you with plenty of time to try out the oysters.

## Directions

1. Walk along the promenade heading north (sea on the right), and at its end, begin the climb uphill on the tarmac road. Very soon the white on red waymarkings of the GR are directing you to turn right onto a little path running around the cliffside. There are several World War II German blockhouses set in the rock beside the path, some now used as bird-watching hides. The path leads

out to a headland known as the Pointe de Barbe Brulée, from which there are good views out into the bay. Ahead of you the Pointe de Grouin can now be seen, and beside it, the tip of the Île des Landes. Continuing from here, the path skirts a camping site and continues through the gorse and bracken alongside the Vieille Rivière, the channel between mainland and island. Keep ahead below the old signalling station to reach paths leading to the Point itself. The whole area is a nature reserve and you are asked to keep to these paths to reduce erosion and preserve the delicate vegetation.

2. When you are ready to return, walk back past the signalling station and again pick up the GR as it leaves the car parking area. The path now runs along the west side where rough moorland covers steep slopes down to the sea. Ahead of you, the point of land is the Pointe du Meinga before St-Malo, and beyond it you can see Cap Fréhel, some 35kms away 'as the crow flies'. The path is easy to follow, and at one point comes up to join the road for a few metres, before descending again into the bracken. At length you arrive above a sandy beach, the Plage des Saussayes.

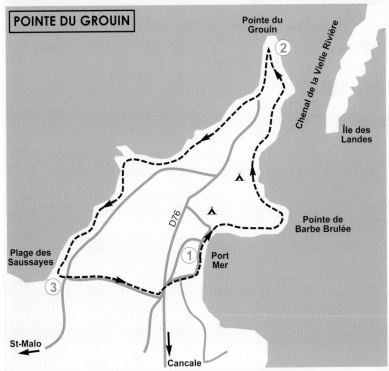

**POINTE DU GROUIN**

Pointe du Grouin

Chenal de la Vieille Rivière

Île des Landes

Pointe de Barbe Brulée

D76

Plage des Saussayes

Port Mer

St-Malo

Cancale

**3**. Do not go down to the beach, but instead bear left uphill to pass a car park and reach the road. Cross this road and continue down the Rue des Tintiaux opposite. From here, turn left into the Rue de la Vielle Rivière, and then cross the main road and head downhill to the beach at Port-Mer.

## More walks in the area

- The coastal path (GR34) offers an attractive section of about 24kms west from Pointe du Grouin to St-Malo, with good places to swim and to visit. A summer bus service between Cancale and St-Malo provides a return option.
- In the other direction, the GR continues along the shores of the bay towards Mont.St-Michel. Le-Vivier-sur-Mer is about 15kms away, but a taxi back will be necessary.
- For a circular walk of about 17kms, take the coastal path from the Plage des Saussayes to the Plage du Guesclin and then divert to the GR34a to head south across the peninsula. At Terrelabouet, turn north along the coast again past Cancale to reach Port-Mer.
- It is possible to take a guided walk out into the bay, visiting mussel and oyster beds, or sand-banks and a bird reserve. The Maison de la Baie at le-Vivier-sur-Mer organises these excursions. (Note that a guide is essential because of the swift tides.)

## Places of interest nearby

- Port de la Houle, the port of Cancale, has an oyster market, and on the edge of the town is an oyster museum, la Ferme Marine.
- At le-Vivier-sur-Mer, 15kms away, it is possible to take a train ride out onto the mudflats to see the mussel 'posts'.
- The village of Rothéneuf is well worth a visit for the 16th century Manoir de Limoelou, once home of Jacques Cartier, who discovered Canada. Here you can see many details of his voyages. The village also boasts some extraordinary rock carvings, the Rochers Sculptés, made by a retired priest in the late 1800s. There are more than 300 carvings of bizarre monsters and rather surrealistic figures on the cliff-face.

**Oyster market at Cancale**

| WALK 3 - Locks on the canal at HÉDÉ | | |
|---|---|---|
| **Length** 6kms | **Time** 1½hrs | **Level** Easy |

**Location & parking:** La Magdeleine, Maison du Canal d'Ille et Rance. From Hédé (just off D137, 20kms north of Rennes) take the Route de Combourg. In about 1km this road crosses the canal at la Magdeleine. The Maison du Canal is on the right, and there is parking on both sides of the canal.

**Refreshments:** good bar/restaurant beside the Maison du Canal; small bar that serves snacks at Bazouges; picnic tables at the start (and finish!) beside the canal.

**Notes:** this is a short and easy walk along good tracks. (Map: IGN Série Bleue 1217 O)

## Introduction

The Ille-et-Rance Canal cuts through from Brittany's north coast to join the River Vilaine at Rennes. Near Hédé the canal climbs through beech woods, eleven locks leading up to its summit section beside an attractive lake. A mere 20kms separates the upper valley of the Rance from that of the Ille. It should have been a simple matter to connect the two - in fact it took more than 25 years and, at one time, more than 1500 workers were employed on the task. In all, 85 kms of canal were created and 49 locks were needed between the barrage at Dinard and the city of Rennes. The canal had originally been a concept of Napoleon, a means of protecting his merchant fleet on the journey from the channel to the Bay of Biscay - from Rennes the journey was completed along the navigable River Vilaine. Napoleon and his troubles were long gone when the canal was finished in 1832.

The canal was in commercial use for over a century, but more recently it has become the preserve of the pleasure boaters. One of the best places for seeing the action is here at la Magdeleine, near Hédé, where locks take the canal up 27m to its summit level, the watershed between the Rance and the Ille. Each lock is accompanied by an old maison d'éclusier (lock-keeper's house). Narrowboats and barges of all sizes travel these waters in the summer months and you can have much fun as a gongoozler (a very English boater's term for those who stand by watching a boat working through a lock - there must be a French equivalent). At the end of the season things are much quieter, but the canal here runs through beech woods making an autumn walk pure joy with its glorious colours.

**Traditional barges on the Ille et Rance Canal, La Magdeleine**

At 65m, the summit is not very high, but those huge locks take away a lot of water each time a boat passes. A large lake was created at Bazouges to maintain the water level, and this has become naturalised and more attractive over the years. After setting out along the towpath, this walk leads you around the shores of the lake, which is a haven for wildfowl - and French holiday-makers! At the village of Bazouges-sous-Hédé you leave the lake and return on quiet roads to the Maison du Canal d'Ille et Rance, itself an old lock-keeper's house which has become an eco-museum with displays and information.

# Directions

**1**. From the Maison du Canal, walk uphill on the grassy towpath beside the canal (water on your right). The path is shaded by huge oaks, with beech on the other side. At the first road bridge, cross over the canal and keep to the wide path under the beeches on the opposite bank. The path continues above the canal with a good view of events in the locks as you go. The GR 37 joins you on this path (white on red flashes on the trees). At the next bridge, again cross the canal, and take the towpath now on its left hand side. Follow this for about 600m and, just after a wooden house on the left, a blue arrow on a tree directs you off to the left.

**2**.Turn left following this arrow and keep to the path through the trees. Soon the path reaches the edge of the feeder channel coming from the lake. Turn left alongside the channel and cross it on the little bridge, working your way back along and above the channel on the other side. The path from here is obvious, and soon becomes a wide track that passes some holiday homes beside the lake. At the junction, do not take the road on the left, but continue along the lake shore on the right. Keep beside this as far as the buildings of le Petit Bourg - about 15 minutes. After passing some lakeside seats and crossing a little bridge and channel, leave the waterside between two old ivy-covered barns and cross the wooden planks over the ditch to reach a small road.

3. Turn left on this road and continue to Bazouges-sous-Hédé. The road comes out beside the church. Now turn left down the main road, and, after about 200m, take the right turn sign-posted to Hédé. Keep to this road for a little over a kilometre, then take a road on the right signed to La Magdeleine. A further few minutes walking will bring you to a T-junction, where you turn left on the main road. Just ahead is the canalside scene at la Magdeleine: boats, locks, picnic tables, bar / restaurant and eco-museum - all waiting to claim your attention.

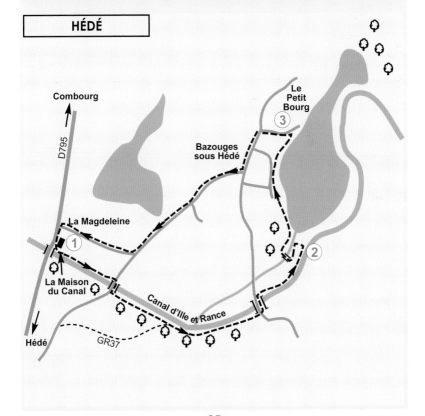

# More walks in the area

- The Maison du Canal at La Magdeleine has details of further walks along and around the canal, including such sights as the town of Hédé itself and an interesting village, St-Symphorien,

  Maison du Canal d'Ille et Rance

  with an ancient manor facing a fine 16th century church.
- There are two linked walking circuits (4 and 5kms) and a TO with further information at Tinténiac, 5kms further north.
- Going east from the Maison du Canal, you have about 12kms of easy walking, following the route of the GR37. There are picnic tables at La Plousière (7kms) and restaurant facilities further on at Montreuil-sur-Ille. To reach this town, leave the canal at the Écluse de Langagé, cross over the bridge and continue along the road for about 1km.

# Places of interest nearby

- The village of Hédé stands on a hill above the canal. It is a watery place, having a large lake on its opposite side and streams tumbling down in all directions. The Romanesque church can be seen for miles around.
- Tinténiac, a small town in a picturesque setting, is 5kms away. Here is the Musée d'Outil et des Métiers - a museum of tools and trades with displays of workplaces, such as a forge and a shoemaker's shop, all in working order.
- The Château de Montmurran, 4kms west, is a medieval castle with a moat, drawbridge and high towers with excellent views.
- The Château de Caradeuc is a fine Regency-style building with park and gardens open to the public.
- The castle at Combourg - grey, turreted and pepperpot-roofed - was built in the 11th century. For a short time it was the childhood home of the Romantic author Châteaubriand, who later wrote evocatively about his austere life there and his room in the haunted 'Cat Tower'.

| WALK 4 - The megaliths of St-JUST | | |
|---|---|---|
| **Length** 13kms | **Time** 3½hrs | **Level** Moderate* |

**Location & parking:** St-Just. From Redon, take the D177 north towards Rennes. After 19kms, turn left where sign-posted to St-Just. Keeping ahead, the church is on the right hand side of the road, and there is a large car park in front of it.

**Refreshments:** there is a bar/restaurant in St-Just, but no other refreshment en route.

**Notes:** walking boots are required, except perhaps in dry weather in summer. *The walk is actually only strenuous on the path beside the lake (clambering over rocks) and the subsequent climb to the moors. With no refreshment available en route, it is advisable to carry fluid in warm weather - and you might like to take your binoculars for the views. The short cut from Point 3 to le Vieux Bourg will cut out about 3kms, but the section missed is particularly attractive. For more details of the megaliths and the flora and fauna of the *landes*, equip yourself with a leaflet (in French) obtainable from the *Mairie* in St-Just before you leave. (Map: IGN Série Bleue 1120 E and 1120 O)

# Introduction

This is an excellent walk in the upper valley of the River Vilaine. Pine woods, gorse and heather, old villages, a lake, and fine distant views all come before the moorland of Cojoux, where a surprisingly diverse assortment of megaliths is scattered over a wide area.

The megalithic site at St-Just has been classified as the second such site in Brittany - and it is mercifully without the crowds found at Carnac. The collection here is quite amazing - menhirs, allées couvertes (gallery graves), barrows, dolmens, and alignments are sprinkled liberally in a landscape of gorse, broom and heather on land known as the Grée de Cojoux. Many of the megaliths have legends attached to them: the Three Demoiselles, huge menhirs, are said to be three maidens turned to stone because they went to play on the moors rather than attend vespers. The Château-Bû, a huge dolmen with chambers and corridors, is rather more sinister - it is said that a young virgin was sacrificed here every year, but fortunately this is almost certainly mythical. At the Croix de St-Pierre, an ancient cross-roads, there are several dolmens and tumuli, and here were found two vases dating from about 5000BC. Perhaps most amazing of all is a semi-circle of rocks known as the

Tribunal - it is actually a prehistoric calendar. The rocks mark the points at which the sun rises and sets at different times of the year when viewed from one distant rock. The tallest rock of all marks the point of sunset at the winter solstice.

The megaliths are a short walk from St-Just, but the whole route described here is well worth taking as it is as gently varied and scenic as any you will find in Brittany. The well-waymarked paths lead you over moorland, through woodland, past tiny hamlets of granite-grey houses, up hills with fine views and into remote valleys with babbling streams. Eventually you arrive beside a most attractive lake in a deep valley and follow its shores for some distance, scaling a few rocky outcrops as you go. A steep climb to the moorland summit follows, and you are on the Grée de Cojoux. Grée is an old Breton word meaning 'height' - and so it is. Wild, windswept and mysterious, dotted with gorse and heather, this is a perfect setting for a remarkable prehistoric exhibition.

**The alignments**

## Directions

1. With the church behind you, walk down to the main road and turn left (D54, direction St-Ganton) At the cross-roads in about 150m, turn right (white on red waymarks of the GR). In a further 250m or so, turn right on a pleasant stony track through pines and gorse. In a few minutes you reach a track junction where the GR leaves to turn left beside the pines. Your route lies straight ahead, now following blue waymarks down the stony track to reach a tarmac road. Here turn left, cross the bridge over a stream, and in about 150m, look for a grassy track on the right. Follow this past a farm on the left. Soon the track corners sharply left, and just after this, you turn right (all this is well-waymarked in blue and yellow) and then keep ahead to meet a narrow tarmac road.

2. Turn left here. Passing a big old granite farmhouse, immediately turn right and continue for about 250m. The waymarks now lead left onto a grassy and stony track climbing uphill. Near the top,

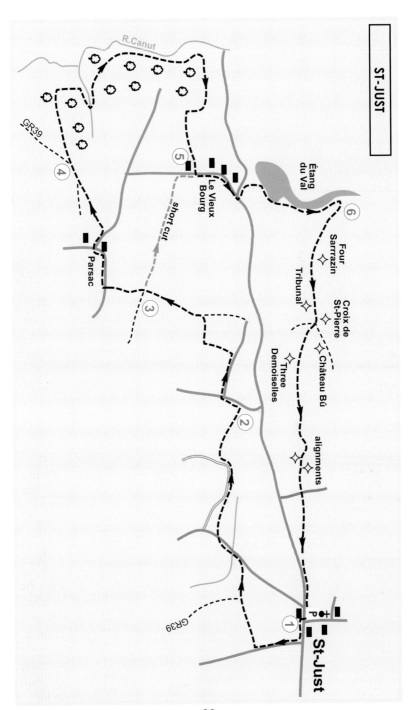

R.Canut

GR39

④

Parsac

short cut

③

⑤

Le Vieux
Bourg

Étang
du Val

⑥

Four
Sarrazin

Tribunal

Croix de
St-Pierre

Château Bû

Three
Demoiselles

②

alignments

GR39

①

St-Just

P

29

turn right and continue climbing towards a spinney on the summit. At the track junction, turn left and skirt the woods on a track from which there are wide views of the moorland to the north. The track descends to a crossroads, and now you have a choice.

> **Short cut:** turn right here and follow the track for almost a kilometre. Turn right at the road and walk through the village of le Vieux Bourg. Here the longer route joins from the left and you pick up the white on red marks of the GR. (Point 5)

3. To continue with the main route, cross straight over at the track junction. On reaching a farm, turn right on the tarmac road and continue on the waymarked route through the beautiful old granite houses of Parsac. At the end of the village, where the road forks, find an open yard on the left beside a quarry. From this yard there are two tracks - take the left hand one, which again is waymarked. This soon leads down through a pretty wooded valley beside a stream, eventually arriving at a wide curving stony track where you continue ahead. A further 100m or so brings you to a track junction.

4. Bear right here. (The GR39 has arrived from the left.) The next very attractive stretch follows the woodland edge and finally arrives in a pretty valley where the river Canut gurgles below on the left. After passing stepping stones and a ford in the river, the path turns and climbs through the wood again. At the crown of the hill, the path winds around a field, and then turns sharply left to descend to le Vieux Bourg.

5. On reaching the tarmac road, turn left and continue through the village. Just before the road junction, there is an old four à pain (bread oven), long redundant. At the junction, turn left and continue on this road for about 50m, to a small car park on the right. Follow the GR up the hill behind it. The path leads on to the landes de Cojoux with the Étang du Val sparkling in its rocky

wooded valley below. The GR marks guide you through the moorland and down to the lakeside, following the bank of the lake, across entrant streams on two bridges. Continue beside the lake for a further 15 minutes, climbing over various rocky outcrops.

**Étang du Val**

**6**. Suddenly the path doubles back, leaving the lake and climbing quite steeply to reach the moorland above. Here there are fantastic views in all directions. The path bears left and soon on the left you see the Four Sarrazin (a tumulus surmounted by an allée couverte) and this is followed by the rocks of the Tribunal. Next comes the Croix de St-Pierre, then the Château-Bû, the Demoiselles and finally the alignments - those beside your path running east-west, others running north-south. This dramatic display of prehistory comes right at the end of the walk, so you can afford to take time over it. From here it is 10 minutes walk back to St-Just. Cross over the road at the end, and follow the footpath across the field opposite. This brings you to the road at the entrance to the village - turn left along it to return to the church.

## More walks in the area

- The GR39 follows the course of the River Vilaine between Rennes and the sea at Pénestin.
- An 18km route from Renac is waymarked in blue, with river valley scenery, water mills, an old chapel, woods and moorland, a fine château and ancient hamlet.
- From Pont St-Marc, a 6km circuit passes through attractive woodland and visits an old hermit's cave.
- The towpath of the Canal d'Ille-et-Rance (from Dinan to La Roche Bernard in the south) provides excellent walking.

## Places of interest nearby

- Monteneuf (on the D776 from Malestroit to Guer) has an exceptional megalithic site, with over 400 stones covering 7 hectares. There is also a 14km circuit visiting other archaeological sites.
- Between Malestroit and Ploërmel, the village of Caro has two megalithic burial sites and la Chapelle Caro has an allée couverte and a dolmen (Dolmen de la Maison Trouée).
- There is a fascinating Musée de la Résistance at St-Marcel, chronicling local life and Breton resistance in the last war.
- The town of Redon is situated on the junction of the Rivers Vilaine and Oust and the Nantes/Brest canal, so a good place for boating or boat-watching.
- The town of La Glacilly is the home of the large Yves Rocher perfume factory, which has a museum and a shop.

**Location & parking:** Tréhorenteuc, on the western edge of the forest, north-east of Ploërmel (follow the D141 for about 13kms). Large parking area in the village, close to the church.

**Refreshments:** pleasant bar/restaurant in Tréhorenteuc.

**Notes:** this is just a short walk, but you can combine it with one of the two walks mentioned below. Trainers would be suitable for this walk in summer, but in winter the paths can be quite boggy, requiring more substantial footwear. (Map: IGN Série Bleue 1019 E)

## Introduction

On the map you will see the Forest of Paimpont - it is in your imagination that you will find Brocéliande, mythical home of King Arthur. The stories of the Knights of the Round Table have their roots in celtic mythology, but they were 'Christianised' and spread by troubadours in the Middle Ages. Chrétien de Troyes told some of the earliest of the Arthurian tales in 12th century Brittany. Forests were always places of legend, and these stories became located here - the Forest of Paimpont became Brocéliande. Here Arthur and his Knights pursued the Holy Grail, but the forest itself has more connections with Merlin, magician at Arthur's court.

Merlin lived not in the court, but in the forest, retiring there to meditate and weave spells. Here you will find the fountain of youth from which he drank, and the magic fountain of Barenton where he met his eternally beloved Viviane. Beneath the lake at Comper he built her a crystal palace, and his tomb is in the woods. The forest is a beautiful place for walking in its own right, but only an incorrigible cynic would deny the sparkle these tales add to the scene. This particular walk is through a beautiful valley on which a spell has been cast by the fairy Morgane - beware!

The walk starts from the village of Tréhorenteuc in the west of the forest. In the middle of the last century, the priest here was one Henri Gillard. He was so absorbed by the Arthurian legends that he began mingling Christianity and mythology in his church. The stained glass windows depict the disciples at the Last Supper - or are they the Knights of Arthur gathered at the round table? The Stations of the Cross have Arthurian themes, while celtic mosaics and legendary creatures decorate the walls. Sadly, his unorthodox ideas were not viewed favourably, and he was asked to leave. He was, however, loved by his parishioners and returned frequently, finally requesting to be buried in the church. This was granted - but how things have since changed! The church has become a place of curiosity, attracting many visitors to the little village. A TO is located opposite and organises conducted tours in summer. Out of season, you can have the key and explore for yourself. A statue of the Rev. Gillard has been erected in front of the main door - he would have been amazed!

Leaving Tréhorenteuc, you head for the Valley of no Return, and it truly is one of the most beautiful parts of the forest. The story here is that the wicked fairy Morgane, half-sister of King Arthur, was betrayed in love, and, in revenge, imprisoned all faithless lovers in this valley. They were condemned to wander for ever in this place, whose entrance and exit were guarded by a rock (Rocher des Faux-Amants) on which sat the fairy herself. Think well before you take this walk! But if you feel you can risk it, there are fine rewards. Deep in the valley is a calm lake, the Miroir aux Fées, at which the fairy folk come to view their perfect reflections, and farther on is a smaller version. A recent addition to the valley is the Arbre d'Or (Tree of Gold), a remarkable sculpture commissioned to commemorate the fire of 1990, which destroyed much of the forest. This valley was replanted by the Association for the Protection of the Val sans Retour. The return is along the rim of the valley with fine views into its deep bowl. Here Merlin would sit at sunset, watching the long shadows creep across the forest - walking here, perhaps you also can feel the magic of this place.

## Directions

1. Facing the church door, turn right onto the road, then right again (on the road to Campénéac). Leaving the village you pass on the left an ancient manor house. Just past it is a large sign directing you left to the Val sans Retour. Climb up the broad stony track and, reaching a barrier ahead, turn right on a track, which is a fire-break, and continue to the left hand bend.

2. Here turn right on a track through the trees, following GR waymarks until you reach a rocky edge amid gorse and heather, where the path begins to descend. On crossing the bridge, the Arbre d'Or is on your right. The sculptor was François Davin, who used the Christian-mythological symbol of antlers to design a golden tree amid the black - life arising from the flames. Continuing, the path leads you around the end of the Miroir aux Fées - the

**Miroir aux Fées**

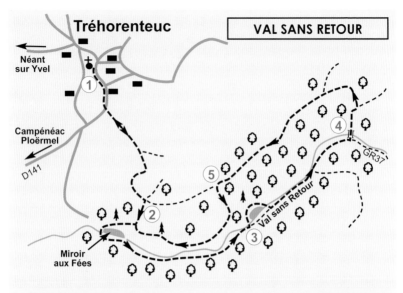

Rocher des Faux-Amants is the red rock high on the left above the lake. Bear left on the path around the lake to enter the valley. Now keep ahead on the obvious path on the right of the stream (Ruisseau du Rauco). After about 15 minutes, you reach a wooden bridge at the end of a second lake.

3. Cross this bridge and continue on the path, which weaves its way through gorse and pines high above the lake. Soon it descends again, and crossing a plank bridge, you now have the stream on your left once more. A signpost shortly appears, and you follow the direction of *la Vallée de l'Aff,* straight on up beside the stream.

4. At a track junction (about 20 minutes from the last lake), the GR37 goes to the right, but you bear left following the yellow waymarks. Cross the stream, and continue to follow the yellow flashes alongside another stream. Bear left again on a track that now climbs out of the valley and rejoins the fire-break. Soon the track levels out and you are above the valley with distant views.

**Sunset across the Valley of no Return**

5. As soon as the view opens out, look for an orange-flashed rock on the left. Take the

**34**

path beside it, which threads through the gorse and the pines to come out along the very rim of the valley. Continue along the edge and you soon arrive at a reasonable track in the right direction. Merlin's seat is one of the fine viewpoints back into the valley. Yellow flashes again appear and lead you across a surface of ridged rock and past another huge boulder to arrive at the GR you started out on earlier. Now turn right, and retrace your steps to the fire-break road, where you turn left to return to Tréhorenteuc.

## More walks in the area

- There are more than 20 circuits in Brocéliande, with information and forest maps available from TOs in Paimpont, Plélan-le-Grand or Tréhorenteuc.
- A 10km circuit, les Landes de Gurwant, passes the superb Château de Trécesson, built of red schist and overlooking a lake. The route also includes a megalith, The Giant's Tomb, and another coffin-shaped prehistoric tomb known as the Maison de Viviane. (This walk connects with the Val sans Retour.)
- An 8km circuit from Tréhorenteuc visits the 'Monks' Garden', a curious flat rectangle surrounded by blocks of stone in alternate colours. Dating from about 3000BC, its true purpose is unknown, but legend has it that a local lord and his hunting party were turned to stone in punishment for taking a monk hostage.

## Places of interest nearby

- The Fontaine de Barenton lies 3kms north, through Folle Pensée. From a small parking area, follow the main path into the forest and the Fontaine is about 1km ahead. The spring is crystal-clear, and rising bubbles of nitrogen give the appearance of boiling. Legend has it that Merlin met the fairy Viviane at the stone slab beside the spring: here she imprisoned him in nine magic circles of air to keep him in the forest forever. It is also said that if, in drinking from the fountain, you accidentally spill water on that stone, a huge storm will arise immediately.
- Travelling on through Concoret will bring you to the Château of Comper. Here, it was said, Viviane was born and raised Sir Lancelot in her crystal palace below the lake. There has been a castle on this site for about a thousand years, and the current château (open in summer) houses the Centre de l'Imaginaire Arthurien, with exhibitions and audio-visual displays.
- The little town of Paimpont in the heart of the forest has an ancient abbey beside a large glassy lake - the perfect spot for a summer picnic.

| WALK 6 - BROCÉLIANDE - Le Château de COMPER | | |
|---|---|---|
| **Length** 10kms | **Time** 2½hrs | **Level** Easy |

**Location & parking:** the Château de Comper. Comper lies on the D31, 2kms east of Concoret. From Paimpont travel north on the D773, and turn right where signed after about 4kms. There is some parking in front of the Château, and roadside parking is possible with care.

**Refreshments:** there are bars and restaurants in Concoret. Light refreshments are available at the Château when open.

**Notes:** the first part of the walk is on a rather overgrown forest track. Do not be put off– it isn't all like this! Later on there are broad tracks with good open views. Trainers should be suitable in summer, but remember that forests are almost always muddy in winter. After about 1¾ hours you should reach Concoret where there is refreshment. (Map: IGN Série Bleue 1018 E)

## Introduction

This gentle stroll in the enchanted forest of Brocéliande, the home of the legendary court of King Arthur, will give you a feel for its magic, before you visit the fairy-tale Château de Comper at the starting point.

The Château de Comper (the original dating from around 1100) was said to be the birthplace of the fairy Viviane, dearly beloved of the court magician, Merlin. Below the waters of the lake he built for her a crystal palace, and here, as the Lady of the Lake, she brought up Sir Lancelot, delivering him to the court of Arthur in his fifteenth year. Few people are allowed to see that crystal palace, and even then for no more than a second. To find out if you will have this privilege, you must come in summer as the château is

unfortunately closed out of season. In winter, all you will see from the entrance is a crumbling turret and an overgrown moat. But if you are here between April and September, you can walk through and see the now-restored castle set

**Château de Comper**

36

beside an enchanted lake with perfect reflections. The château now houses the Centre de l'Imaginaire Arthurien - an exhibition of tableaux and videos that will acquaint you with the legends and their place in the forest.

The legends associated with this sector of the forest are not particularly Arthurian, but there are plenty of those to be found elsewhere, as you will learn from the exhibition in the château. The walk heads off through quite

One of the three Roches de Trébran

thick woodland and soon comes upon three huge boulders known as the Roches de Trébran. Apparently they dropped from the aprons of fairies on their way to build Mont.St-Michel - in the absence of any better explanation for their presence, but they must have been pretty strong fairies! Farther into the forest, there is suddenly an abundance of tropical plants. In the last world war, this was the site of a German camp, whose commandant was a keen gardener and nature lover. He had his camp planted with rare specimens, many from conquered or allied countries - some have lived on here for over half a century. After passing Concoret, an attractive village with a fine church of purple granite, it is an easy return on clear tracks to reach the château with its legends. If you remember that the lake is only a mirage, with luck you will glimpse that crystal palace beneath!

## Directions
1. From the Château de Comper, follow the road downhill towards the lake. At the fork before the lake, you should turn left (signed Muel), and keep to this road for about 200m to a sharp right hand corner. Ignore an obvious track going off to the left; take instead another track on the left a few metres farther on - a much overgrown track through gorse and broom. It is marked by a faded blue flash on a telegraph pole. This narrow path continues uphill through the bushes for about 1km, finally arriving at a hard-surfaced clearing, the junction of several tracks.

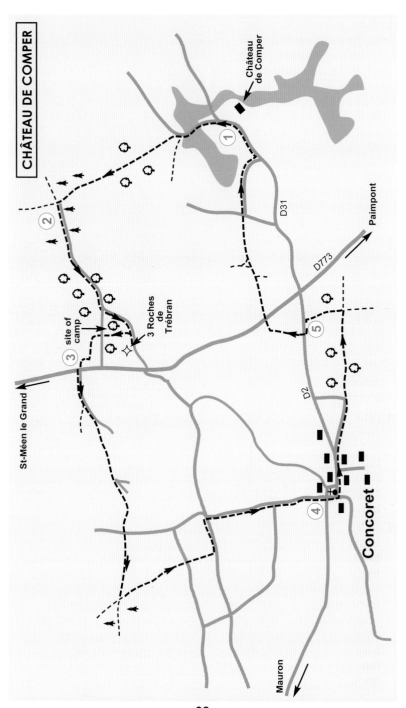

38

**2**. Turn left downhill and follow the road for about 800m. After a right-hand bend there is a barrier on the road ahead. Here turn left and follow the hard track downhill. Soon the track bears right, and almost immediately afterwards you see a blue arrow urging you to turn right. If instead you continue ahead for about 50m here, you come to the rocks known as Les Trois Roches de Trébran, hiding in the forest on the right. Now return to that blue arrow at the junction and follow its direction uphill. The concrete rectangle beside the junction is the remains of the swimming pool at the German camp. Continue uphill past the ruined buildings of the camp, where you can still see surviving vegetation obviously alien to the forest. After two cross-tracks, an arrow on a tree directs you left. Soon turn right to reach the camp entrance, and then left to the main road.

**3**. Cross straight over the road (signed la Feuvrais). First bear left, then at the fork, leave the tarmac road, keeping right. After about 700m, bear right at a sort of T-junction and shortly arrive at a tarmac road. Cross straight over and head uphill towards the pine wood. At the cross-tracks before the wood, turn sharp left and continue downhill with very pleasant views for about 10 minutes. Several tracks are crossed as you go, but your track keeps straight ahead towards the church at Concoret and is clearly waymarked. Cross a small tarmac road, and on reaching a second, turn left (church spire now on the right). At the cross-roads, turn right towards Concoret.

**4**. Arriving in Concoret, you have the church on your left. Turn left around the church wall and keep straight ahead, following signs to Comper and blue waymarks. About 250m from the church, turn right at a cross-roads. Soon this road itself bears to the left, but you continue ahead following the Circuit de Comper with its blue flashes. At a big cross-tracks with fine views to the right, turn left.

**5**. At the tarmac road (250m), turn left. After about 100m, turn right beside a house (there seem to be orange dots rather than blue here). Continuing ahead, the track turns sharp right and comes to a main road. Cross straight over to the broad earthy track opposite. After a track on the right is passed, you arrive at a track junction. Here you take the track bearing away to the right (a farm is seen in the distance ahead). After about 300m, cross a narrow tarmac road and continue ahead past the farm. The road now bears right past other houses and farm buildings to reach a larger road. This is the D31 and here you turn left for about 250m to reach the Château de Comper.

Part of the old Château de Comper

## More walks in the area

- For general walking in the forest with its fine oak and beech trees and many lakes, see note at the end of Walk 5.
- A 12km circuit from the village of St-Malon-sur-Mel passes an old stone quarry, an ancient menhir and an alley grave known as the 'Tombeau des Anglais' as well as the more famous sites of Merlin's Tomb and the nearby Fontaine de Jouvence, from which Merlin drank to preserve his youth. Apparently if you gaze into the waters for just one minute, this should be sufficient to remove wrinkles - provided you have bare feet at the time.
- In the north of the forest are two attractive areas - the lake and woods of Trémelin and the dramatic Valley of the Chambre du Loup (locally described as the Grand Canyon!). There are several marked routes in this part of the forest.

## Places of interest nearby

- The Château de Comper with its exhibitions and bookshop is worth a visit (seasonal opening).
- The lake of Trémelin has a recreation area with small sandy swimming beach, pedaloes, canoes and other boats. There are also other sporting facilities and an excellent bar/restaurant.
- The small town of Paimpont in the heart of the forest has a stunning 12th century abbey church in an exceptional lakeside setting. The original monastery here was founded in 645 by the Breton King Judicaël.

See also the notes at the end of Walk 5.

# Loire-Atlantique

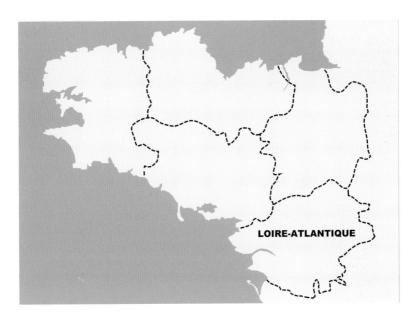

**Brière Regional Park at sunset**

# WALK 7 - Mills and Muscadet at MONNIÈRES

| Length 10kms | Time 3hrs | Level Easy to moderate |
| --- | --- | --- |

**Location & parking:** the church at Monnières, which is just south of the N249 (E62) a few kilometres east of Nantes and is signed from that road.

**Refreshments:** none on route but some in Monnières.

**Notes:** trainers adequate in summer, but out of season tracks by the river can be muddy. Little shade on route.
(Map: IGN Série Bleue 1324 O)

## Introduction

South-east of Nantes, two rivers wind their way through a rolling landscape of vineyards. The rivers are the Sèvre and the Maine, and though there are few visitors to this area, the product of those vineyards is very well-known: Muscadet. The first vines were planted in this area by the Romans. These were ultimately destroyed by marauding Vikings, but the vineyards were replanted in the Middle Ages and thrived until the particularly severe winter of 1709. When spring came, the only grape variety to have survived was the Melon de Bourgogne, the Muscadet grape, and so the vineyards were replanted with that resistant 'cépage' and became renowned for their production of Muscadet.

In 1881, all the vineyards of France, and indeed Europe, were destroyed by phylloxera, an American beetle that attacked the

**Windmill in a vineyard**

roots of the vine. Only American vines were unaffected, but it would have been sacrilege to plant French vineyards with American vines. The problem was solved by grafting the French Melon de Bourgogne on to immune transatlantic rootstock, and so Muscadet is still produced here today.

At the replanting after the phylloxera crisis the vines were set in rows for the first time in order to improve access for the workforce. Even today many of the tasks are still carried out by hand. Every vine is individually pruned over the winter months, a truly mammoth task, and in this area almost half of the harvesting is still manual. The whole story of Muscadet is told in the Musée du Vignoble Nantaise at nearby le Pallet, which is well worth a visit after the walk.

This walk is certainly about the vineyards, but it does have other ingredients. An attractive riverside path at the start, a Grotte de Lourdes, a deer park, a lake, an ancient bakehouse and a couple of windmills are just a few. One of the windmills, the Moulin de la Minière, has an old staircase taking you to its upper floor, from where you can view the vineyards rolling away into the distance, and attempt to count the 23 church spires said to be scattered among them.

## Directions

**1**. From the church, walk downhill (signed Saint-Fiacre). Where the road corners left, keep straight ahead between houses and barns to enter a vineyard. Turn briefly left, and then go right, on a clear path between the vines. Reaching a wall on the right (after passing the end of a small road), look out for a left turn through the vines (occasional yellow-on-red GRP waymarks on the stones of the track). To the right, the houses on the far bank of the Sèvre are Port Domino, the quayside where wine was once transhipped. At a cross-tracks go straight ahead, cross a footbridge and bear right alongside a stream to arrive on the riverside in front of playing fields.

**2**. At the river, turn left. Then leave the river and cross between the football pitches. Behind the pavilion, ignore the road climbing steeply, but turn right on a track through the woods. Reaching the Grotte de Lourdes in the cliff, descend the steps and keep to the riverside, next passing a plantation of poplars before arriving at a tarmac road.

**3**. Turn left on the road and climb the hill. Past a large field with a lake on your right, a road joins from the right, but you continue to the top of the hill where the road swings left. At a cross-tracks here, take a broad track doubling back through the vines on the right. After about 150m, turn onto a track on the left leading to the windmill on the hilltop, the Moulin de la Justice. When you reach it you will have a fine view over the village of Monnières.

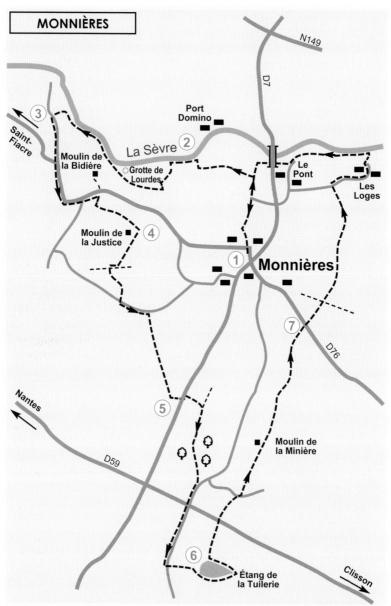

MONNIÈRES

N149

D7

Port Domino

Saint-Fiacre

3

La Sèvre 2

Moulin de la Bidière

Grotte de Lourdes

Le Pont

Les Loges

Moulin de la Justice

4

1 Monnières

7

D76

Nantes

5

D59

Moulin de la Minière

6

Étang de la Tuilerie

Clisson

**4**. The track bends to the right across the front of the windmill and then descends a little to meet a broad track. You are now in the middle of a vast vineyard and may be wondering how you are going to get out. Not to worry - turn right on that broad track and very shortly (with the windmill on your right), there is a track on the left that will take you all the way down to a tarmac road. Turn left and after about 5 minutes (when the road is climbing out of a dip), find a clear track through the vines on the right. A wood and a windmill can be seen ahead and to the left. The track corners left just before reaching the road.

5. Cross the road and take a track about 20m along to the left. At a T-junction of tracks, go right and continue through pleasant woodland. Eventually you reach another small tarmac road on which you turn right to meet the busier D59. Cross this latter road with care and take the road opposite for about 300m. Then a gravelled track on the left leads to the Étang de la Tuilerie, where there are inviting picnic tables beside the lake shore.

6. If you now walk in an anticlockwise direction about three-quarters of the way around the lake, you will find another gravelled track leading back to the D59. Another careful crossing will have you on a broad track leading directly to the Moulin de la Minière at the top of the hill (a little tarmac road is crossed en route). When you arrive at the windmill you can enjoy the amazing panorama of vineyards from its summit, and see that behind the mill a statue of Notre-Dame is keeping careful watch over the crops. When ready to continue, maintain the same direction on a broad track that in about 15 minutes reaches a main road.

7. Cross to the track opposite. Keep straight ahead over cross-tracks to reach another road (approx. 15 mins). Turning right here will take you into the hamlet of Les Loges, where the road bends downhill towards the river and then continues as a footpath. Following this, you can bear right to gain the wooded track along the riverside. Soon the path reaches the hamlet of

Le Pont, where an alley on the left leads between stone buildings to the old square with its *four banal* (communal bakehouse), a sight well worth the diversion.

**Four banal, Le Pont**

Returning down the alleyway, many lovely old stone buildings are passed before reaching the river-bridge. From here the main road will quickly return you to the church, but if the river is low enough, you can escape all that noise and traffic by continuing under the bridge as far as a wall blocking the path. A left turn up the bank here will bring you back alongside the wall in the vineyard through which you passed at the start of this walk, and you can simply retrace your steps to the church.

## More walks in the area

- A GRP of this area (about 90kms), which would provide several days of walking, starts in Nantes and follows the Sèvre south to Clisson before returning along the Maine valley.
- From le Pallet, a 7km route (Circuit de la Sanguèze) starts at the Chapelle St-Michel, passing the Musée du Vignoble Nantaise in its course.
- There is also an 8km circuit from le Pallet with lots of wine-related interest. The route passes through Port Domino (where once wine was loaded into flat-bottomed boats to be taken into Nantes) and continues to Le Pé-de-Sèvre, a village of old stone houses with external staircases.

## Places of interest nearby

- The Musée du Vignoble Nantaise is on the edge of le Pallet, above the valley of the Sanguèze. Vines of old varieties are planted on the terraces around the building and the museum displays wine-making equipment, past and present. Wine tasting is also available.
- The town of Clisson has a 12th century fortress-château and a covered market dating from the Renaissance. The town was rebuilt in Italian style following its destruction in the turmoil of the Vendée uprising after the French Revolution.
- The Château de Goulaine, 10kms north of Monnières is a stone, slate-roofed building which has been in the same family for over a thousand years. As well as visiting the house and a greenhouse of tropical butterflies, it is also possible to buy the estate Muscadet.

# WALK 8 - Loire and ocean at ST-BRÉVIN-LES-PINS

| Length 14kms | Time 3½hrs | Level Easy |
|---|---|---|

**Location & parking:** the *Ancre de Marine* (a ship's anchor) on the sea-front at St-Brévin-les-Pins, which is south of St-Nazaire, across the bridge over the Loire. Head for the town centre, not St-Brévin l'Ocean, and from there to the sea front, where you will see the anchor. Park on the front or nearby.

**Refreshments:** plenty in St-Brévin and by the estuary.

**Notes:** all on good tracks and minor roads, but no shade.
(Map: IGN Top 25 1123 OT)

## Introduction

The Loire is France's longest river - more than 1,000kms separate its source high in the Cévennes from its mouth on the Atlantic coast near St-Nazaire. And, fittingly, that longest river now slides silently into the sea under the gracefully-curving Pont de St-Nazaire, which at 3,356m is France's longest bridge.

The walk here is on the opposite side of that estuary, where the holiday promenades of little St-Brévin-les-Pins offer a complete contrast to the docks and oil-tankers of the city. From the town itself, a network of tracks and minor roads leads you past the holiday villas to a somewhat neglected path beside the grey waters of the estuary. The scene is brightened by the long line of carrelets, rather rickety raised fishing platforms from each of which dangles a square net that can be lowered into the water at the appropriate tide. Most are graced with a cheerfully painted shelter for the fisherman.

Beyond the elegant bridge, the carrelets give way to a harbour of fishing boats, and holiday-makers stroll along the shores - you

'Fruits de mer' for sale in St-Brévin market

47

have clearly returned to civilisation! At the point itself, a maritime museum now occupies the fort built here by Vauban, which is strangely tucked into the lee of high banks. You can climb them to reach an orientation table, and look out over the mingling waters of river and ocean. Then it's south along the Atlantic shore, and a completely new perspective with golden sands, blue waters and pine trees ahead. St-Brévin is a delightfully unsophisticated resort and if you have time to spend here, this region at the mouth of the Loire has a lot more to offer than you might expect.

## Directions

1. From the Ancre de Marine, cross the road and walk up the Rue de l'Église and into the Place de la Victoire. Continue in the same direction across the main road, past a parking area and into the Rue Albert Chassagne. The statue of Our Lady at the end of this road was erected here in fulfilment of a pledge made by the residents of St-Brévin during the worst air raids of the Second World War. Continue from here under the fast road, and then uphill for about 500m.

2. Turn left on the Chemin du Grand Ruau. Pass a narrow road on the right and then take a track on the right heading for the water-tower. Just past the tower you reach another tarmac road. Turn right and then almost immediately left on a track into a field. A not-too-impressive menhir by the name of Pierre du Plessis-Gamat stands on the right. The track eventually bends right to reach a metalled road.

> **short cut:** to reach Point 6 directly - simply turn left on the road and stay with it to the junction (approx. 800m).

3. To continue with the main route, cross this road and then another immediately afterwards, to reach the Chemin des Rochaffais. This road takes you past a German Blockhaus and then corners left to a T-junction. Turn right here (still on the Chemin des Rochaffais) and at the next junction turn left on the Chemin des Grinchais. Ignore tracks branching off on the left and continue to the hamlet of La Haute Prinais.

4. Turn left here and then after about 100m right, beside a white garage. This track now takes you through to the village of la Grand'Ville. At the road junction, turn left passing the Ferme des Abeilles (Bee Farm) to reach the pond and picnic tables under the pines in the centre of this attractive village. Keep straight

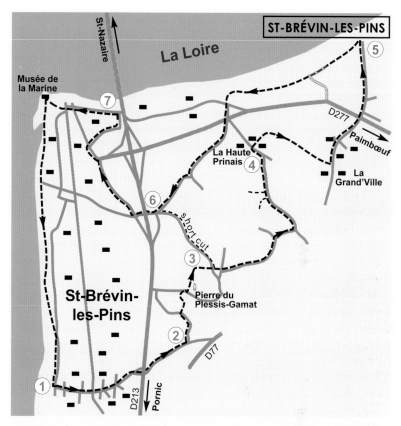

ahead here to meet the busy D277 and cross it (with care) to take a road opposite leading down to the estuary.

5. This is the place to admire all those spindly fishing platforms lined up along the shore. When you are ready to continue, go left on the road behind the factory, which then becomes a sandy lane. Where the lane veers left (after 500m), walk ahead on the track, crossing rough ground parallel to the estuary with a fine view of the bridge ahead. In 10 minutes or so, you reach a tarmac road and can turn left to meet the D277 again. (Turning right instead of left here looks a short cut on the map but it crosses the extensive campus of a hospital and can't be recommended.) Cross the D277 to a road opposite and stick with this as it bears to the right around an area of marshy ground to reach a road junction (approx. 15 mins).

6. Bear right, walk under the fast road, and at the next junction turn right in the direction of Mindin. At the next road junction

keep ahead (ignoring signs to Paimbœuf) and then take the next road on the right, the Avenue des Fosses. This latter road bends to the left to come out at the foot of the St-Nazaire bridge. Now continue ahead on a footpath running up to the main carriageway, but just before reaching it, turn left and drop down to the promenade above the beach.

**St-Nazaire bridge and the Loire**

7. Keep straight ahead to the point with its Musée de la Marine, from where you can take a last look at the rather muddy waters of the Loire. Then turn south and follow the pleasant path above the beach all the way back to the sea-front road and the Ancre de Marine.

## More walks in the area

- South of St-Brévin, a blue waymarked circuit of 15kms starts from La Plaine-sur-Mer and goes right round the very attractive stretch of coastline at Pointe de St-Gildas.

- For some unusual walking in the summer months, the Brière Regional Park (across the bridge to the north), has raised paths through the peat marshlands. Two interesting routes start from the Port de Bréca, including a 4km walk past the picturesque Port de Tréhé.

## Places of interest nearby

- Paimbœuf was the main port on the Loire until the 18th century. From this old shipping centre it is possible to take a cruise as far as St-Nazaire. Just to the east of Paimbœuf, a canal constructed at the end of the 19th century to take larger vessels to Nantes can still be seen.

- North of the Loire, try a drive along the peninsula to Le Croisic, and then on to the salt flats. The Maison des Paludiers at Saille has all the information about salt-working in the area.

- The Brière Regional Park not far away is more than worth a visit. Here it is possible to hire flat-bottomed boats and punt off into the reedy wetlands, or for an easier option, take a guided trip. There are also well-preserved old villages in this area, with many reed-thatched houses.

# Morbihan

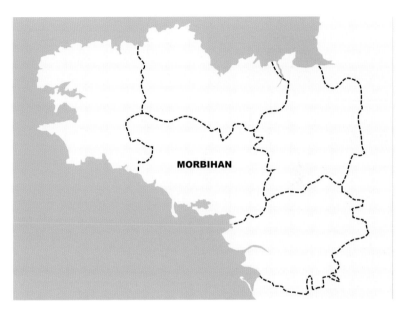

Fontaine de Ste-Barbe, Le Faouët

| WALK 9 - Beside the River Ellé at Le FAOUËT | | |
|---|---|---|
| **Length** 12kms | **Time** 3hrs | **Level** Moderate |

**Location & parking:** the town square at le Faouët, which lies just off the D769, some 40kms north of Lorient. All roads lead to the town square, where there is plenty of parking.

**Refreshments:** eating places of all kinds around the square at le Faouët - although the choice is more limited out of season.

**Notes:** not a particularly difficult walk, but there is a short scramble up rock to the viewpoint over the valley. Trainers should be adequate in summer, but out of season walking boots would be preferable. The walk is largely in the woods, making it very suitable for a hot day, but take fluid with you.
(Map: IGN Série Bleue 0719 0)

## Introduction

Le Faouët is well-named, 'faou' being an old Breton word for a beech tree. This walk climbs through the beech woods beside the 'chaos' of the tumbling River Ellé to reach the 15th century stone chapel of Ste-Barbe, perched on rock high above the river.

The countryside around le Faouët is termed the Pays de Roi Morvan after the Breton King Morvan who was here defeated in battle against the Franks in the 9th century. The Bretons were always a rebellious crew, and Morvan was just one of a succession of leaders who physically opposed Frankish domination. The land that now bears his name must be one of the most attractive - and little known - parts of Brittany. This is the Argoat, the forested country of the interior, and here among rushing rivers and wooded hillsides it seems that every village possesses a medieval building of some note. Chapels, manors, halls, abbeys and water-mills are scattered liberally across the rolling landscape.

Le Faouët itself is a most pleasant small town, and boasts a vast covered market hall, dating from the 16th century, set in an attractive tree-lined square.

Outside the town are magnificent woods of beech and oak, and a steep valley where the little River Ellé tumbles over a 'chaos' of boulders in its rocky bed. This is fine walking country, and the local rambling group has waymarked several interesting circuits in the area. On their recommendation, this walk combines the best of them - and will almost certainly tempt you to try others.

This walk is excellent at any time of year, but on a sunny autumn day the colours are quite stunning, the burning amber of the beeches contrasting with the deep greens of the undergrowth and mossy rocks. Reaching a bridge over the Ellé, you climb steadily beside the rushing river on a path meandering through the trees to emerge at a rocky view point high above the valley. After passing a pumping station at the head of the valley and doubling back along its top edge, with fine views all the way, you plunge back into the woods, to come upon an ancient fountain and then the ornate, gothic-style chapel of Ste–Barbe itself. It seems a strange place for such a fine chapel, but the story goes that in 1489, Jean le Toulbodou, a local landowner, was out hunting here when a severe storm broke. Lightening split the rock face beside him, and in terror he prayed to Ste-Barbe to take care of him. She did - and in gratitude he built this grand edifice. Should you too be here in a storm (apparently this place attracts lightening) you can invoke the blessing of Ste-Barbe by tolling the bell in the bell house at the top of the steps. From the chapel, an old paved pilgrims' path through the woods takes you back to the town below.

**Beside the Ellé in autumn**

## Directions

1. Leave the central square via a narrow road from the middle of the north side, opposite the covered market - the Rue des Halles. Cross the road at the top and continue ahead on the Chemin de Ste-Barbe. Soon you are on a lovely wide high-banked path beneath the trees that leads you down to a tunnel under the express-way. Crossing under this to the far side, turn immediately right following the direction of the Circuit du Chaos. This path continues for about 500m through the woodland above and parallel to the express-way. The path then clearly bends left away from the road and after a further 300m brings you to a fork. Here do not take the path left into the wood, but go straight ahead and descend to the road beside the river bridge.

2. Walk along the road to the bridge and, just before it, take the track on the left, signed with a yellow flash on the Circuit des Chapelles. As you approach an old mill, the track forks and you bear left above the mill, following the signs. Continuing uphill on

this track through the woods another signpost is soon reached, and here you turn right following the direction of the Circuit du Chaos. Winding your way through the waymarked trees, you arrive at the riverside. The path from here beside the rocky river is quite delightful, and you follow it for some 3kms, climbing gently all the while. At one point some big rocks bar the way, but the yellow flashes direct you to keep left and climb them. A fine view across the valley awaits you at the top - it's also a good spot for a picnic. Descending again on the waymarked path you once more follow the river, which after a while becomes calmer, while the path beside it widens as it passes through a plantation of pines. The path then leaves the river and climbs again to reach the white buildings of the pumping station.

3. Just after the pumping station, ignore the waymarks directing you to the right. Instead, continue ahead on the road which doubles back as it climbs above the pine wood. In about 400m, after passing the stone buildings of a farm on the right, turn left, following the sign to the Circuit du Chaos back down into the wood. The path now runs high on the side of the valley, and, after again turning uphill, emerges on the top with views all around. Gorse and bracken line the path and soon a fingerpost directs you through them to a viewpoint. Continuing again, ignore a path to the Ellé going off to the left and go on to a tarmac road at a small hamlet.

4. After passing between farm buildings, turn left following another Circuit du Chaos signpost. Passing more viewpoints, you arrive in about 500m at a major track junction. Here the Circuit du Chaos goes off to the right uphill, but you leave it and follow instead the track ahead towards Ste-Barbe. Almost immediately, at another fork, follow the direction 'Fontaine' (now ignoring Ste-Barbe). A further 250m or so along this track brings you to another fork with a broad path going uphill to the right. This is the Pilgrims' Path leading up to the chapel - but, behind you, it continues downhill to reach the Fontaine, a spring where clear bubbling water arises in a well-head dating from 1708.

Return from the Fontaine on the Pilgrim's Path where soon the grey eerie bulk of the Chapel of Ste-Barbe appears through the trees as you climb. Through the archway, steps lead uphill to the bell house on the edge of a flat plateau with distant views. The custodian's house is nearby and at holiday times it should be possible to view the interior of the chapel where there are fine stained glass windows.

**5**. When you are ready to leave, walk along the edge of the field away from the bell house. Continue ahead past the barrier at the wide gap in the wall and alongside the next field. Stones begin to appear in your path, and very soon you are on a cobbled track dipping into the woods. This is again the Pilgrim's Path, which then descends quite steeply and, just before the express-way, passes some converted farm buildings which now house the Musée de l'Abeille Vivante - a bee museum. The picnic tables outside look inviting, but if you prefer to eat in town, keep ahead and retrace your steps under the express-way to return to the square at le Faouët.

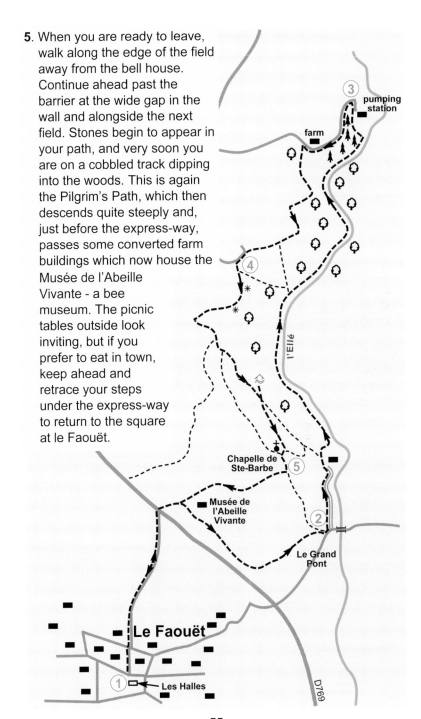

# More walks in the area

- Of the local routes, there is a very attractive 10km one, the Circuit de Saint-Sébastien, following the valley of the River Ellé. Another choice would be the Circuit de Diarnelez (10.5 kms), which visits the ancient manor of that name above the valley of the River Inam.

- To the east of le Faouët and the Ellé is another pretty valley, that of the River Scorff. The route that climbs through the wooded valley of the Scorff to St-Auny is most picturesque and passes chapels, ancient villages, water-mills and many fine viewpoints. This attractive part of Brittany seems quite unknown – and is ideal for discovering on foot!

# Places of interest nearby

- If you are interested in ancient chapels, you must surely start at St-Fiacre, just south of le Faouët. This 15th century chapel, with fine stained glass windows, is best known for its magnificent carved and painted rood screen, depicting in the most graphic form the seven deadly sins. At St-Nicholas, just to the east, there is another fine rood screen.

- More medieval gruesomeness is revealed in the remarkable 15th century wall paintings at Kernascléden (10 kms east), and there are more notable chapels at le Croisty and St-Tugdual, St-Caradac-Trégomel and Berné. At Langonnet you will find an abbey with an original chapter house dating from the 13th century.

- For more active pursuits, there are lakes for sailing and swimming at Priziac, Langoëlan, Plouray and Langonnet, and the Ellé and the Scorff are great rivers for fishing. South of Meslan is wild country known as the Roches du Diable where the Ellé crashes through a wooded gorge with fine viewpoints. More walks are possible, along with fishing, mountain biking, canoeing and other activities.

**Chapel of Ste-Barbe**

## WALK 10 - The golden cliffs of PÉNESTIN

| **Length** 13kms | **Time** 4hrs | **Level** Easy |
|---|---|---|

**Location & parking:** the TO just south of the town centre at Pénestin. Pénestin is on the Atlantic coast between Vannes and La Baule. Follow the N165 east from Vannes and leave at La Roche Bernard (signed Pénestin). At the roundabout just before the town, turn left. The TO is on the right and there is plenty of parking outside.

**Refreshments:** several bars and restaurants in Pénestin, with particular emphasis on Fruits de Mer.

**Notes:** suitable for trainers in dry weather. Extending your walk along the estuary about a kilometre will bring you to the port of Tréhiguer, where you can visit the mussel museum and find refreshment. Most of the route is exposed.
(Map: IGN TOP25 1022 OT)

## Introduction

The little resort of Pénestin sits at the southern edge of Morbihan where the River Vilaine meets the sea. This walk is one of contrasts - high cliffs along the sea coast, salt marshes in the estuary, and inland the bocage, the ancient Breton countryside with its high-banked tracks.

Pénestin is an out-of-the-way sort of place. It is cut off from the rest of Morbihan by the wide estuary of the Vilaine and from the land to the south and east by the great marsh of the Brière. A little farther along the coast is the modern resort of La Baule, but its sophistication has not rubbed off on Pénestin. This is a pleasant and unspoilt little town which, despite some very fine beaches has rarely found its way into the guide books.

It must have been something of a shock to the inhabitants when, at the end of the 19th century, Pénestin was found to be sitting on gold. A gold mine was opened near the town, but the venture was short-lived, the returns were poor, and at the time of the First World War the mine was closed down. It remains only in name - the nearby popular beach is the Plage de la Mine d'Or, where, interestingly enough, the sandstone cliffs at sunset glow with the colour of the precious metal. Along these cliffs, then, the walk sets out, and you have views of the rocky coast and small islands out to sea as you go.

Moving onwards, there are more fine beaches before reaching the rocky Pointe de Halguen and the estuary. Oddly, it is the estuary rather than the sea that has supported Pénestin's economy through the ages. For many centuries, sea salt was harvested here, and along the estuary you can still see the rectangular pits where sea water was circulated and evaporated by sun and wind

**The golden cliffs at sunset**

to form the crystals of salt. This all ceased at the end of the 19<sup>th</sup> century and since then, mussel farming (la mytiliculture) has become an important industry. The fine quality of the mussels is said to be due to the oxygenated water mingling with the sea water in the estuary. At low tide, look out for rows of buchots - the posts where mussels collect. At Tréhiguer, a little farther along the shore (you can extend your walk) the old lighthouse has been converted to a 'mussel museum', and is well worth a visit. The route returns to Pénestin on quiet roads and sunken lanes, past a manor house and over a hill with a view. Once back in town, there are several good sea-food restaurants where you could check out the quality of those mussels!

## Directions

**1**. From the TO, walk down the road away from the town to the roundabout. Here turn right to reach the Sports Hall. Walking behind the Sports Hall, you reach a path which runs between the football pitch and the tennis courts. At the end of the football pitch, turn right on the grassy track. In about 100m (just around the corner), bear left at a junction of sunken tracks, and in about 15m, bear left again at another junction. The track now bears right and passes to the right of the houses to reach a tarmac road. Cross this to the track directly opposite. At the fork in front of a house, bear left. Soon you arrive at the cliff-top path. To the left you can see the Plage de la Mine d'Or with its golden cliffs, and beyond it, a rocky promontory with a little island (Île de Bel Air). Much farther out is the larger Île Dumet.

**2**. Turn right on the cliff-top path. Below you is a glorious sandy beach, ahead is the Pointe de Halguen at the mouth of the

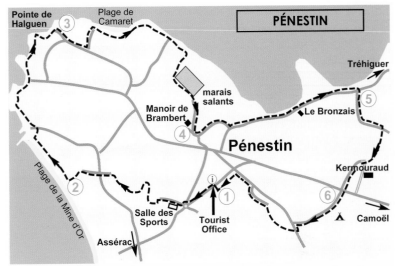

estuary and behind it, the whole south coast of Morbihan. Gorse and pines line the path. At the end of the cliffs, you find yourself in dunes above rocky outcrops as the coastal path continues around an attractive curving bay. As you reach the point, the waymarks direct you away from the coast around the fence of the building at the end. Returning to the coast, a seat under the pines gives a fine view across the mouth of the estuary.

3. On reaching a small road coming down to another little beach (Plage de Halguen), turn right following the green arrow. Bear left at the top and then follow this road for about 300m, to where a road on the left takes you down to the Plage de Camaret (green flash on telegraph pole). This is another attractive little beach, after which some more climbing leads you to the Plage de Menard. Here you are in a wide grassy area beside the estuary. Ahead are the marais salants - the old salt pits - and if you fancy an adventure it is possible to pick your way between them and the sea. But the safer route turns inland here along a broad grassy track between pines and gorse. Waymarks direct you to bear left and you follow along behind the salt marsh, crossing a little bridge over an entrant stream. The path approaches the town and reaches a junction (old Manoir de Brambert on right).

4. Turn left here and shortly, at a T-junction, left again following the colour flashes on the Rue de Lienne. At the end of this road, turn left on the wider road. On your left is a pleasant area of

pines and picnic tables alongside the estuary - you could choose to leave the road and walk on the far side of them instead. Again on the road, continue through the village of Le Bronzais.
(**Diversion**: If you wish to visit the village and port of Tréhiguer with its mussel museum and bar/restaurant, it is just 1km farther along the road.)
Otherwise, turn right on the Route de Berniguet - there is a green flash on the corner.

5. The Route de Berniguet bears sharp left, and then slightly right where the road begins to climb again. Here take the track on the right between high banks - there should be a green waymark at its entrance. Continue on the tree-lined track with good views of the estuary to the right. Ignore all side tracks until you pass a lake on the right and see farm buildings ahead (Manoir de Kermouraud). Now keep to the right hand track which winds round and uphill to come out at a tarmac road. Here continue ahead to reach the main road shortly.

6. Cross directly over the main road to the road opposite. This skirts a campsite on the left and descends, bearing right to a road junction. Here turn left, and after about 30m, turn right on a track where again there is a green waymark. The track joins a road beside some new housing and this road continues, bearing right to reach a main road. Turn left towards the church, but just before the end of the road, turn left on a track called Chemin de Lavoir. Bearing right at the end of this brings you to the main road where the TO is just opposite.

**Across the estuary of the Vilaine**

## More walks in the area

- From Pénestin, follow the coastal path south along the cliffs for approx. 7kms as far as the Baie du Bile. At high tide this is a very pretty bay; at low tide it is a hive of activity with shellfish farmers going about their business in the oyster and mussel beds.

- A short circular waymarked walk from Camoël (about 6kms east) will take you past the attractive port at the Barrage d'Arzal, the dam which cuts off the tidal portion of the Vilaine.
- The navigable part of the River Vilaine has a walkable towpath beside it for much of the way – it connects with the Rance north of Rennes, so you could actually walk to Dinan! There are also many interesting circular walks along its valley.
- The GR39 approximately follows the Vilaine from Rennes to the sea providing many further possibilities for linear walks.
- The Brière Natural Park (south-east of Pénestin) is a must to visit in this area. This is an ancient land of marshes and canals where peat-cutting and reed-gathering are traditional occupations. Walking is possible here only between June and September, but there are several waymarked paths and the strange light across these marshes makes walking a magical experience.

## Places of interest nearby

- See text of the walk for the port, restaurant and mussel museum at Tréhiguer.
- Two small museums provide further information about the harvesting and collection of sea salt: the Maison des Paludiers at Salle near Guérande (about 25kms south of Pénestin) and the nearby Musée des Marais Salants at Batz-sur-Mer. Salt is still harvested from the bay south of Guérande, where you can see a vast patchwork of salt pans and drainage channels, much beloved by wading birds of all kinds.
- If you feel like exploring the Vilaine by boat rather than on foot, there are daily trips up that river from the barrage at Arzal. Everything from a simple trip to a 4 hour dinner cruise by candlelight is on offer.
- To the south and east of Pénestin is the Parc Naturel Régional de Brière, a vast area of marshland and reeds crossed by canals (see 'More walks' above). Here several 'ports' offer you the opportunity to hire one of the local flat-bottomed boats and take yourself off into the wilderness for the day. If you are afraid of getting lost, you can opt for a guided trip instead. It is truly an area of outstanding natural beauty, but there are other tourist attractions in the form of many preserved old houses and villages in the local style.

| WALK 11 - A tour of the Île d'Arz | | |
|---|---|---|
| **Length** 16kms | **Time** 4hrs + | **Level** Easy |

**Location & parking:** the harbour (Cale de Beluré) at the northernmost tip of the Île d'Arz.
An inexpensive ferry service operates 10 times a day in winter and 13 times a day in summer. You can catch the ferry 3 miles south of Vannes at Conleau (from the centre of Vannes, follow signs to 'Le Port' and 'Conleau') or, if coming from the east, at Barrarac'h (follow signs to the town of Séné, then Port Anna and Barrarac'h). The trip takes about 20 minutes.

**Refreshments:** hotel/restaurant at the harbour; bar/restaurant near the eastern causeway; restaurant, crêperie and a shop in the town (le Bourg). Not all are open in winter.

**Notes:** walking boots not necessary. Much of the walk is quite exposed - in summer, protect yourself from sun and carry water. Swimming possible. Take binoculars – the views are magnificent! Last boat of the evening is usually quite late - but can be very punctual. (Map: IGN TOP25 0921 OT)

## Introduction

The peaceful, green Île d'Arz has the best views of the Golfe du Morbihan. This interesting walk follows the coastal footpath, with sea-views all the way - and plenty of opportunities for a swim.

The Île d'Arz has the sort of outline you might expect from an ink drop splashed across a page. Fingers of land reach out into the sea giving promontories each with a different view, and between them, curving sandy beaches and tiny coves. Some outlying reaches of land are connected with the main island only by causeways, one of which is backed by an interesting tide-mill. The island is fortunately less popular than its neighbour the Île aux Moines, where seasonal crowds are attracted by the fine residences and tropical vegetation. The Île d'Arz remains a more simple place of fields, sea and sky, the height of its civilization being the tiny granite town at its centre. You can have a peaceful walk even in the middle of summer. Out of season, although the ferry still runs hourly, you may well have the island pathways entirely to yourself, although the bar/restaurant in the little town is open all the year round, as is another restaurant on the island. This walk is made special by the ever-changing views as you move around the island. The Gulf of Morbihan has proverbially 365 islands - although the number changes with the state of the tide! You can see almost all of them from some point around the shores of the Île d'Arz. The shallow sea is speckled with boats, ferries and wind-surfers heading in every direction.

One of the advantages of island walking is that it is difficult to get lost. The coastal path is a grassy track almost all the way - only rarely will your feet touch tarmac. The route is mostly open, although the southern tip has magnificent tall pines that shade the site of a megalith and make a fine picnic spot. There are several excellent beaches - being an island, you can always find a sheltered one whatever the wind's direction. The shallow water on the western side has been dammed to provide power for a tide-mill, while on the east there are old marais salants - rectangular pits once used for evaporating and collecting salt from the sea. There is an old manor at Kernoël and a 17th century church in the town.

**Houses in the bourg**

# Directions

1. From the slipway (la Cale), walk past the hotel/restaurant and continue down the road, ignoring the Sentier Côtier signpost on the left. Pass a campsite on the left and skirt the wide sandy beach on the right. Across the water past some little pine-topped islands, you can see the Île aux Moines, the largest island in the Gulf. Ahead, the Pointe de Berno projects far into the sea.

2. At the end of the beach, leave the road beside some conifers before the first houses of the town. Keep beside the shore on a broad grassy track taking you out to a pine-clad promontory ahead. Reaching the tip of this, in front of you is the low wall of the Étang du Moulin - a lake much favoured by wading birds, where skeletons of long-dead boats project from the marsh. On the wall is a tide-mill. The path runs behind the étang and crosses a causeway to reach a piece of land that is virtually an island, where you continue with the shore on your right to reach the Pointe de Berno. Of the islands to the north the largest is Île Drennec, while far to the northwest, beyond the Île aux Moines, the Pointe d'Arradon on the mainland reaches out into the sea.

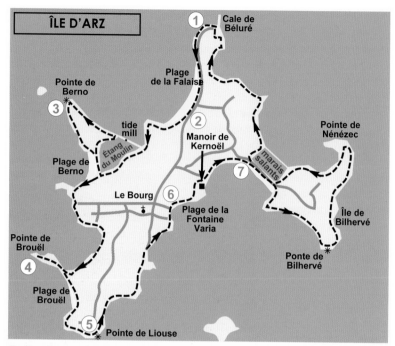

**3**. Continue along the western shore, crossing the causeway with the Plage de Berno on your right. Keep ahead past the little harbour with its slipway, to reach a rocky coastline, from which obvious tracks will lead you into town if you wish. Continuing beside the coast, follow a Sentier Côtier sign to the right, skirting the bay to reach the Pointe de Brouël ahead. A narrow strip of land takes you out to its rocky tip, where a shrine hides among the gorse bushes.

**4**. Returning over the causeway, a picnic-table and seats are well-placed for a break in the journey. The Plage de Brouël (now on your right), backed by rocks and pine trees, is probably the prettiest beach on the island, recommended for bathing. Ahead is the southernmost tip of the island, the Pointe de Liouse, a fine viewpoint where the remains of a dolmen are hidden beneath a canopy of tall green firs. From here you are looking south into an arc of islands - the largest, ahead and to the left, is the Île Ilur - and beyond them is the coast of the Rhuys peninsula near Sarzeau. The southern tip of the Île aux Moines hides the end of that peninsula and the exit from the Gulf to the open sea.

**5**. After the Pointe de Liouse, the path swings north to run along the cliffs, for a while bordered by thorn hedges, towards the town again. Approaching the little harbour, there is a sailing school and then a pleasant picnic site. Past the slipway, a track to the left beside some tall conifers leads up into the town. (If you want to explore the town follow this track uphill, until you reach the square with its bar/restaurant. To regain the coastal path, turn right behind the restaurant and keep straight ahead.) To continue on the coastal path, carry on beside the beach (ignoring signs to the embarcadère unless you want to return the 3kms by road to the port).

**6**. Bear left, and, emerging through a barrier behind some houses, turn left on the track to reach a metalled road. Ahead of you is the old, grey Manoir de Kernoël. Turn left on this road and in about 20m, right, into a field. The path skirts the fence of a property to reach a track leading to the sea. Turn left here between houses to reach a metalled road beside a restaurant proclaiming itself 'Open all Year'. Continue along the road for about 200m to a T-junction, and turn right towards the causeway.

**7a**. Cross to the Île de Bilhervé (if you are running short of time or energy, you could omit this part of the walk - the tour around the island will take you nearly an hour). There is a good beach, and a good viewpoint at the Pointe de Bilhervé. Farther on, the path wanders up to the Pointe de Nénézic where a little granite house sits on its own island. The path then follows beside a wide marsh popular with all manner of sea birds at low tide. Returning to cross the causeway again, you have a fine beach on one side and the marais salants on the other. Sea salt was harvested here from the Middle Ages until about a hundred years ago.

**7b**. Continuing from the causeway, follow the Sentier Côtier signpost, which takes you past marshland at low tide. The path continues round the coast until, just as you think you have reached the harbour, it takes a sharp left turn into a field. The road is soon reached, where turning right will take you back to the harbour.

**Ferry from Conleau arriving at the Île d'Arz**

# More walks in the area

- The Île aux Moines, with more houses and tropical vegetation than the Île d'Arz, makes a good day's outing. The path here is not exactly circular, more up and down and sideways, but there are more than 20kms of footpaths and some lovely beaches. Catch the ferry from Port-Blanc.

- From the end of the Quiberon peninsula there is a boat service to each of three islands out in the sea. The largest of these is Belle-Île-en-Mer, which has a beautiful long coastal footpath. The other two, the islands of Houat and Hoëdic, each have a coastal footpath that can be walked in three or four hours. Hoëdic is the smaller and more wild, whilst Houat is perhaps prettier with fine cliffs, coves and beaches.

- There is just one other major island off the coast - the Île de Groix, this time reached by ferry from Lorient. The island has a waymarked coastal path, which will take about two days to circumnavigate.

- From le Hézo on the eastern side of the Gulf follow the coastal path (here a GR with white and red waymarks) south via St-Armel to Lasné. The path crosses oyster beds in the ancient marais salants. From St-Armel you can walk out on a causeway to le Passage and from Lasné you can walk out to the Île Tascon if the tide is low.

# Places of interest nearby

- The TO in Vannes can provide you with a good map of the area around the Gulf and also a town map, which will guide you around the picturesque walled old town area - ancient ramparts, old lavoirs, a covered medieval market, and the cathedral with its cloisters and fine formal gardens.

- The island of Gavrinis near the sea entrance of the Gulf is well worth a visit. In summer, boats cross from Larmor Baden on the west coast. This tiny place has one of the most remarkable megalithic sites in Brittany, a tumulus so large that it is the highest point in the Gulf. Beneath a grass-topped stone cairn, a long corridor, its supports decorated with ancient carvings, leads to a burial chamber dating from about 4000 BC.

- Another remarkable megalithic site is Carnac, on the coast just west of the Gulf. To the north of the town is an amazing collection of alignments in various sites - the ones at Kermario have nearly a thousand stones in ten rows. The whole area is scattered with menhirs, tumuli and dolmens and is a must if you are anywhere in range.

# Côtes d'Armor

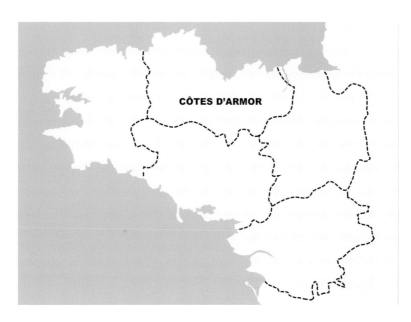

CÔTES D'ARMOR

**River Blavet at the Abbaye de Bon Repos**

## WALK 12 - Rocky shores at Lac de GUERLÉDAN

| Length 6kms | Time 2hrs | Level Moderate |
|---|---|---|

**Location & parking:** Mûr-de-Bretagne, the Rond-Point of the Lac de Guerlédan. Mûr-de-Bretagne is just south of the N164 between Loudéac and Rostrenen. The Rond-Point is on the lake, 1km west of the town (follow signs to *Centre Nautique*). There is good parking at the Rond-Point.

**Refreshments:** none on route. There is an attractive bar/restaurant at the Rond-Point with views over the lake, and another bar on the approach road, but neither is open in winter. Mûr-de-Bretagne is a pleasant little town with good restaurant facilities of all kinds.

**Notes:** suitable for trainers in dry weather in summer. At other times walking boots are advised. (Map: IGN Série Bleue 0818 E)

## Introduction

Hurrying by on your way to the beaches of Finistère, you may just have glanced south from the busy N164 near Mûr-de-Bretagne and glimpsed a landscape of forested hills and deep valleys, and among them, the waters of the Lac de Guerlédan. Set in wooded hills at the heart of Brittany, this lake has an almost alpine feel to it. For holidaymakers it offers sailing, canoeing, swimming - and walking! This short ramble gives you just a taste of the many waymarked routes in the area.

The Suisse Breton is a term that the tourist board has used for this area, which is certainly overstepping the mark a little. Nevertheless, it is very attractive, and a far cry from what most British holidaymakers think of as a Breton landscape.

The Lac de Guerlédan is almost entirely surrounded by woodland that reaches to its shores and spills over the cliffs of grey granite and schist. Surprisingly, this picturesque lake is man-made, formed some 60 years ago when the Blavet, like so many other French rivers, was dammed to provide hydro-electric power. The Blavet here was part of the Nantes to Brest Canal, a waterway created by Napoleon to bypass the attacks of the British fleet in the Bay of Biscay. The canal has more recently been turned over to pleasure craft, but Guerlédan now effectively splits it in two, and boaters must content themselves with half a canal to east or west. The lake attracts a different kind of boating in its own right - in summer a medley of canoes, dinghies, windsurfers and trip-boats ply the waters.

The shores offer other attractions - you can hire a pedalo or play mini-golf, go for a swim or build sand castles on the beach. You can also take a walk! The woods around are laced with trails and circuits and indeed, a GR encircles the whole lake. Farther back, the wooded slopes are cut by gorges where rivers tumble spectacularly to end in the waters of the lake or the River Blavet.

The walk chosen here is just a short one and follows the shores of the Anse de Landroannec at the eastern end. The lake is said to have the shape of a dragon from the air - in which case, you are walking around its head. The route first follows the GR beside the lake and through the Bois de Cornac - fine woods of beech, chestnut and oak. The return is an easy walk along the route of an old railway line with good views of the surrounding countryside. Back at the Rond-Point you can enjoy a meal overlooking the lake, or if you fancy a swim, take a 5 minute drive to the pretty beach at Caurel.

**The beach at Caurel**

## Directions

**1**. Take the path that heads into the woods to the right of the Basse Nautique buildings. You will see the white on red markings of the GR on the trees. Continue up beside the fence and at the top bear left, and again to the left at the site board. There is a fine view here and a Parcours Sportif runs alongside your path at this point. At the end of this, at a fork, bear downhill to the left towards the lake. Continue on a very scenic path above and beside the lake, following the GR waymarks through woods of beech, oak and holly, where occasional seats are placed to tempt you. Eventually the well-signed path leaves the shore and climbs up to a Village de Vacances.

**2**. At the tarmac road, turn right and then immediately left to cross the car parking area. At the far side of this, beneath the electricity lines, a path leads down beside the field to reach the lake again. At the lakeside (there is a fine beach to the left), turn right and continue beside the lake with open views. At the first junction, beside some wooden buildings, turn left and keep ahead on the road, passing the end of the lake and a picnic site.

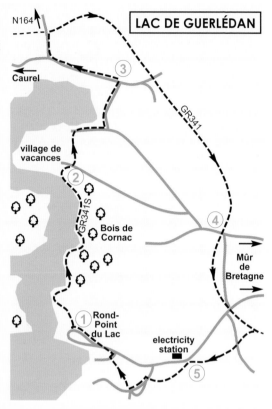

3. Leaving the lake, turn left at the T-junction. At the next junction, in about 400m, turn right away from the lake. This road junction is also a junction of GRs, the point where the main GR341 (which you are now going to follow) splits into North and South versions to encircle the lake. After walking uphill for about 150m, turn right onto the gravelly track of an old railway, again marked with white and red flashes. This is a most pleasant track, shaded along its length by beech trees, and with good views.

4. After about 1½kms, the old railway track crosses a wide tarmac road. Here the GR341 leaves you and turns left into the town. You continue ahead on the railway track, now marked with yellow flashes. The track passes under a road, and about 200m after this you should take a path leaving the railway and doubling back on the right (yellow arrow on tree). In a further 200m, cross over a tarmac road and continue ahead with woods on your right and views to the left.

5. On reaching another tarmac road opposite an electricity station, do not join it, but rather bear left on a waymarked track behind the hedge. This soon bears right and becomes a broad grassy track leading uphill. Where this reaches another metalled road,

turn left uphill to reach a junction at a corner. Now turn right on a track beside a house (waymarked) and continue through the woods downhill. Cross over a track and continue downhill again. Almost immediately,

**Lac de Guerlédan**

bear left, again following the yellow flashes, on a wide track towards the lake. On reaching the road at the bottom, turn right and then left to return to the Rond-Point.

## More walks in the area

- The walk around the entire lake is about 48kms, but there are several places to stay en route and take two days over it.
- The area to the north of the lake includes some spectacular gorges and megaliths as well as forest walks. The 11km Circuit des Landes covers moors, woods and the Beau Rivage beach on the lake, with swimming and refreshments available.
- To the south, the countryside is similarly pleasing and there are various colour-coded routes around St-Aignan. A circuit marked in orange, for example, passes the barrage, the Chapel of Ste-Tréphine and the site of Castel-Finans, said once to have been the castle of the ferocious Baron Comorre.

## Places of interest nearby

- The lakeside beach area of Beau Rivage is just a few kilometres away - leaving the Rond-Point for Mûr-de-Bretagne, turn left where signed. Here there are camp-sites set in woodland above the water, a most attractive sandy beach, restaurants and trip boats for taking tours of the lake.
- The barrage presents a different aspect from the car-park above St-Aignan. The huge concrete slope at the back is quite terrifying. In July and August there are free tours here to find out how water generates power.
- In St-Aignan there is a tiny electricity museum - a curious diversion, but only open in summer.

## WALK 13 - BON REPOS and the GORGES du DAOULAS

| Length 5½kms | Time 2hrs | Level Strenuous |
|---|---|---|

**Location & parking:** Bon-Repos Abbey, which is right in the centre of Brittany, just south from the N164 at the western end of the Lac de Guerlédan. Park where signed for the abbey, beside the road before it crosses the river.

**Refreshments:** hotel/restaurant and a café at the abbey, bar/crêperie beside the bridge over the Blavet, and a bar beside the main road. Plus all facilities in Guarec, 5kms west.

**Notes:** the path up to the megaliths is steep - and the one down even steeper, as well as rocky. Add to this the ridge-top walk, and you can see that good footwear is needed - walking boots preferable. Take water on a hot day - you will appreciate it after the climb - and binoculars as there are excellent views from the top. (Map: IGN Série Bleue 0818 0)

## Introduction

This walk climbs from an old abbey beside the river Blavet to a high plateau of granite and schist. These are some of the oldest hills in the world, formed in the primary era, about 600 million years ago. Here, three remarkable ancient burial chambers conceal themselves amid the gorse and bracken, high above the Gorges du Daoulas.

The walk starts at Bon-Repos Abbey, a 12th century Cistercian establishment beside the River Blavet. The descriptive name was inflicted by its founder, Alain, Vicomte de Rohan, an insomniac who finally achieved a good night's sleep here after a day spent hunting in the nearby forest. Leaving the abbey, you are soon climbing quite steeply up the sides of the gorge. Reaching the plateau at the top you are in the *lande*, a landscape of gorse, broom, bracken and heather, quite wild, remote and very attractive. Hidden here, each in its own clearing, are the three Allées Couvertes de Liscuis, some of the best-preserved megaliths in the area. Out of season the spot will almost certainly be deserted, and it can be quite a mystical experience to walk beside these ancient tombs on a misty morning, alone on the roof of Brittany.

Allées Couvertes, or gallery graves, are the most elaborate of the megaliths, like a row of tables forming several chambers each having a purpose - one was an entrance hall, others were tombs and another contained objects needed in the after-life. The whole was then covered by an earthen mound or a cairn of stones. There are many such megaliths in this area and the explanation lies in the local discovery of a quarry of fine granite and a 'w o r k s h o p' producing 'polished' axes, all dating from the Neolithic era, some 5000 to 2000 years BC. Axes from

**Allée couverte above the Gorges du Daoulas**

this quarry have been discovered all over France. To the north of the quarry was found an area of habitations, and to the south, an area of tombs.

Moving on from the megaliths, the path becomes more demanding as you follow a GR beside the edge of the plateau. Here jagged teeth of quartz project along the rim of the gorge and, in the typical style of a GR, every crest is visited for you to appreciate the view. The ridge-top path and the subsequent descent into the gorge make this a walk not for the faint-hearted. But eventually the road is reached, and you return through the gorge beside the rushing river.

## Directions

**1.** Walk up to join the main road and turn left along it (with care!). Immediately after crossing over the River Daoulas, a road on the right is signed to the Gorges du Daoulas. Ignore this and take the next road on the right a few metres further along. This road climbs and bends to the left. Ignore the first track off to the right just after the bend - even though it has GR waymarks - and continue for about 100m to another track where a granite sign points to the Allées Couvertes and is waymarked in yellow. The path first climbs gently through woodland where little sign-boards offer you the opportunity to learn the names of trees in French. After this it climbs quite steeply, passing an old quarry and the site of a slate-workers' hut. More climbing brings you to an information board telling you about the flora and fauna in the *lande* - you have a chance of seeing fox, badger, deer and even wild boar up here. The views are superb, and extend as you climb.

**2**. Reaching a cross-tracks at the summit, a granite sign on the left
describes the features of the allées couvertes. Walking past it
for 200m or so, you arrive at the first of these impressive
megaliths. Its setting is equally impressive, with views for miles
across the coloured distant hills and wooded valleys. Continuing
past the megalith, you reach another and turning sharp right
here, a third. The track past this shortly brings you to a sort of T-
junction where you turn right to reach a wooden signpost (just
before the original track junction with the granite sign, Point 2).
Now you turn left, following the direction of the GR341 towards
Caurel. The GR is well-marked with the usual white and red
bars and is easy to follow.

**3**. After about 300m, look out for a right fork - the path ahead is
marked with a cross. Soon follows a fine ridge-walk, the path
marked with both yellow and white on red waymarks that lead
you on past various rocky outcrops with magnificent views.
Eventually the path turns and makes a dramatic descent down
the side of the gorge.

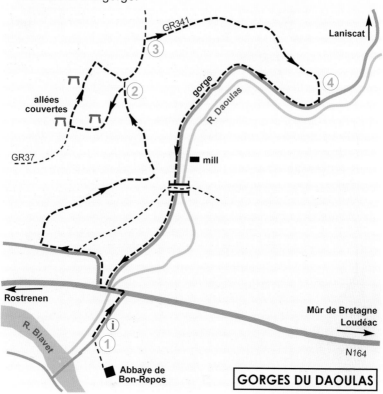

GORGES DU DAOULAS

74

**4.** On reaching the road, turn right and follow it through the gorge and past the old water-mill - now ignoring all waymarks persuading you to turn left. Continue instead to the main road, and here turn left and retrace your steps to the abbey.

**In the Gorges du Daoulas**

## More walks in the area

- To the east, an 8km circuit from the pretty village of Saint-Gille-Vieux-Marché follows the granite Gorges de Poulancre.
- From Plussulien, 12kms to the north, a 9km walk includes the site of the afore-mentioned Neolithic axe-quarry at Quelfenec.
- At Maël-Carhaix to the west there is a 4.5km circuit including a sunken path deep in a valley, where the vestiges of a Roman aqueduct are pointed out on wayside signs.
- The ancient Forêt de Quénécan to the south of Bon-Repos has many marked walking trails which are colour-coded. There may be restrictions of access in the hunting season as deer and wild boar are at home here.

## Places of interest nearby

- Bon-Repos Abbey dates from the 12th century, was re-built in the 14th century and destroyed in the Revolution. Now there are only ruins, but along with them you can enjoy various craft workshops and exhibitions. A trip boat operates cruises along the canal from the river bridge.
- Cross the river bridge and follow signs to reach Les Salles des Forges, the site of an old iron and steel works opened by the Rohan family and dating from the 18th century. The setting is impressive - beside the pool and ruins of the château once belonging to the Rohans, you can visit the restored iron worker's house, the chapel and school.
- The village of Laniscat is known for its fine 16/17th century church with a rare carillon of 25 bells, and an old quarry-worker's house in blocks of granite. Further on is the chapel of Saint-Gildas with its three fountains - one for men, one for women and one to protect dogs from rabies!

## WALK 14 - The Pink Granite Coast at PERROS-GUIREC

| Length 14kms | Time 4hrs | Level Easy |
|---|---|---|

**Location & parking:** Perros-Guirec on the north coast, midway between St-Brieuc and Morlaix. Park at Plage de Trestraou, to the west of the town.

**Refreshments:** many bars and restaurants at both the Plage de Trestraou and at Ploumanac'h. Also in the village of La Clarté.

**Notes:** these are well-trodden paths and small roads – trainers would be quite adequate footwear, except for the diversion into the valley of the Traouïero (see direction 5). There is little shade on much of this route. On a hot day, think of protection from the sun and carry fluids. Swimming is possible - the best beach is that of St-Guirec at Ploumanac'h, although the tide goes out a long way. For looking at off-shore islands take binoculars!
(A booklet *Discovering the Footpaths along the Coast of Ploumanac'h* is available from tourist offices.)
(Map: IGN TOP 25 0714 OT)

## Introduction

This has to be the most amazing of Brittany's coastal walks, following the Sentier des Douaniers, the famous coastal path from Perros-Guirec to Ploumanac'h, and returning inland with many fine views. The coastal section itself is 6kms in length, and it is possible to make the return (or outward) journey by bus.

West of Perros-Guirec, the rocks of the Pink Granite coast take on the most bizarre of profiles, their rounded deep-coloured forms contrasting boldly with the azure sea. The 'Pink Granite' rock is, in its natural state, a sort of dusky red colour and here the erosion of many millennia has rounded its corners, worked deep fissures and generally been the architect of the most eccentric of sea-scapes. This is a popular holiday area, and the path is well-known, so you are unlikely to have the scene to yourself. Nevertheless, this is a walk that should not be missed and you can always enjoy a little more solitude on the return route.

Leaving Perros-Guirec on the broad well-sign-posted track, you may, at first, wonder what all the fuss is about. The wide bay stretches before you, limited by a few humps of orange-glowing rock. Arriving at that rock, you are in a cove known as Pors Rolland - and the walk takes on another dimension. From here the rock formations become more fantastic by the minute. Many have been given names - the foot, the chameleon, Napoleon's hat - but

**Pors Kamor**

you can readily invent your own. The rocks of the Squewel tumble out on a peninsula into the sea and various others perform the most astonishing acts of balancing. The unworldly scenes continue, and reaching the cove of Pors Kamor, surrealism seems to have finally taken over. Here is a deep round pool of turquoise sea surrounded by grotesque shapes of darkest browny-red. Nearby is a lifeboat station, and, not far away, a lighthouse from which you can see the full length of this colourful coast. These shores are now a conservation area and the Maison du Littoral at Pors Kamor has a permanent exhibition.

St-Guirec beach, although not without its rocks, seems something of a haven in this pageant. Behind the perfect horseshoe of its shores is the little town of Ploumanac'h where you can find welcome refreshment. Beside the beach is the chapel of St-Guirec - he landed here in the 6th century, having crossed from Wales. Not far away, on rocks on the shore, stands the tiny oratory of St-Guirec, a shelter containing a granite effigy of the saint. Legend has it that in addition to his healing skills he was adept at finding husbands. Any maiden who wishes to marry within the year has only to stick a pin in the nose of the saint - but even granite cannot withstand such onslaught, and the unfortunate St-Guirec is now without a nose.

After the harbour at Ploumanac'h the route turns inland, passing above the valley of the Traouïero. Since Traouïero is

Breton for 'Valleys', this seems to be the Valley of Valleys! And well it may be, since this is a most attractive place filled with dense woodland hiding more huge rocks of pink granite beside a tumbling river. A diversion into its depths is possible - but you may feel it merits more time on another day. The pink granite quarries themselves are passed as the route climbs to the village of la Clarté with its historic chapel. The final treat is the viewpoint with its orientation table at la Tertre, from where there is a fine panorama over the whole coast.

## Directions

1. From the western end of the Plage de Trestraou, a signpost to the Sentier des Douaniers directs you uphill on the road. As the road swings left, the coastal path leaves on the right. From this broad track there are now distant views of the pink granite outcrops ahead, and of the Sept Îles, the string of islands out to sea (only five!). Coming up to the first of the rocks, the path forks, and you bear to the right towards the coast. Soon you are in Pors Rolland, a most attractive cove guarded by a fissured rocky outcrop known as 'The Castle'.

2. Pors Rolland marks the start of the curious rock formations. Following along the coast you soon reach the Devil's Rock, falling abruptly into the sea. Odd rocks are poised precariously on others - The Bottle and The Sea-Tortoise - and those projecting into the sea form the Squewel peninsula. A customs officers' lookout hut is passed and behind rocks the tiny powder store for canons protecting the coast. Out to sea, on the Île aux Moines, you can just see the outlines of a Vauban fort. Soon

**powder store**

78

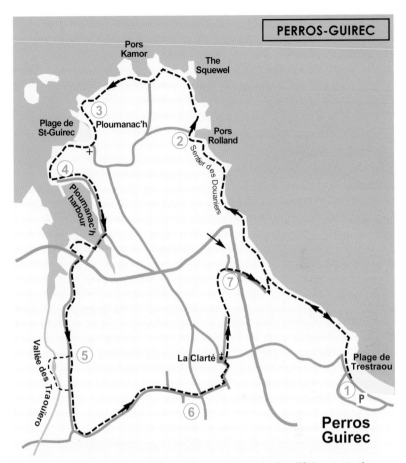

you reach the cove of Pors Kamor. Here is the lifeboat station and the Maison du Littoral. Beyond is the lighthouse, and eventually the path turns inwards through an area of tropical vegetation to reach the beach of St-Guirec.

3. As you reach the beach, the chapel and oratory of St-Guirec are across the bay ahead. Follow this around, walk through the confines of the chapel and continue on the obvious path following the white on red bars of the GR. The path climbs up through rocks and then descends with good views of the château on the Île de Costaérès. This château was designed by a Polish architect and it was lived in for a time by Henryk Sienkiewicz, who completed writing his novel Quo Vadis in this strange place. The path continues to the harbour at Ploumanac'h.

79

**4**. Follow the road around the harbour to the far side, and then leave it to cross the estuary on the dam, passing the tide-mill. Continue following the waymarks around the edge of the estuary to reach the road beside the bridge. Now leave the GR and turn left along the road. Take the first road on the right (approx. 100m), signposted to the Site des Traouïero. This road climbs and passes through a village. After about 500m, on the right, there is a sign board telling you of the paths in the Valley of the Traouïero.

**5**. (If you wish to sample the valley, follow the path here to the bottom, cross the river before the lake, and keeping left, cross back on the second bridge after the lake. Keeping uphill on this path, you will rejoin the road some 400m farther along.)

The main route continues along the road with views (and sounds) of the pink granite quarries to the left. After about 500m, turn left at the first road junction and descend towards them. The road passes the entrance gates, and continues to climb towards La Clarté.

**6**. Reaching a cross-roads in the village, cross straight over on the Rue de Triagoz, and at its end, turn left. Next bear right and then left to arrive at the Chapelle de la Clarté. The story is that in the 14th century, the Marquis de Barac'h was returning from the English coast with his fleet. A thick mist engulfed them and they were carried towards rocks they could not see. The Marquis prayed to the Virgin Mary, and promised her a chapel if she would save them. A ray of sunshine broke through showing them the land. Faithful to his word, the Marquis built the chapel of Notre Dame de la Clarté at the place illuminated by that shaft of light.

Pass behind the chapel (keeping it on your left), and, coming to a road, cross straight over onto the Rue du Tertre. Soon you arrive at the viewpoint in a wide grassy area on the left. There are fine views from here. Keep ahead on the track, ignoring tracks on the left and finally reach a narrow tarmac road. Here turn right to come down to the main road.

**7**. Cross the main road and take the Rue des Fougères, approx. 30m down on the right. This descends quite steeply, soon reaching a track junction, where you double back to the left to reach the coastal path again. Turn right and retrace your steps to Perros-Guirec.

**Rocks of the Pink Granite Coast**

## More walks in the area

- Follow the GR34 coastal path for 5kms more to Trégastel, or even for 20kms to Trébeurden. Bus connections are possible for the return - ask at the TO.

- The Valley of Traouïero is quite spectacular, with huge granite boulders, caves, viewpoints and rare vegetation. There are route information boards and a leaflet is available from TOs.

- West of Trégastal, the Île Grande (beaches, viewpoints, a bird centre and allée couverte) can be reached by causeway for a 7km circular walk on the coastal path.

- Circuits at Pleumeur-Bodou and Trébeurden (latter 8kms) pass a variety of prehistoric megaliths, including several menhirs (one in the sea).

## Places of interest nearby

- The Maison du Littoral at Pors Kamor has information about granite and the curious rock formations. Open mid-June to mid-September.

- Radome at Pleumeur-Bodou. This gleaming white sphere is the headquarters of the French Telecommunications research, with a daily English version of its latest technology show. The museum has many hands-on exhibits and the Planetarium de Bretagne is nearby.

- The Sept Îles provide an off-coast bird sanctuary with many rare breeds including puffins. Accessible by boat from Perros-Guirec and Ploumanac'h in season, landing is on the Îles aux Moines, with its lighthouse and Vauban fort. There are also seals in the vicinity.

## WALK 15 - woods above the estuary of the TRIEUX

| **Length** 12kms | **Time** 4hrs | **Level** Moderate |
|---|---|---|

**Location & parking:** Site de Frinaudour. From Paimpol, take the D15 south-west to Plourivo, and continue on the D82 through Penhoat to the estuary. Park at the end of the road.

**Refreshments:** none on route or nearby.

**Notes:** mostly on good tracks, suitable for trainers in dry summer weather - walking boots at other times. Most of the walk is through shady woodland - good for a hot day. Some climbing and descending involved, but nothing too strenuous. Take food and lots of fluid with you. The return is across attractive moorland, but you can catch the train back from the halt at Lancerf. Times available from the TO at Paimpol or at the stations, Frinaudour, Maison de l'Estuaire, Lancerf - all request stops - you just flag down the train! It does work, but if your walk would be spoiled by doubts, first catch the train to Lancerf and walk back either way. (Map: IGN Top 25  0814 OT)

## Introduction

This is a walk along wooded slopes high above the estuary, with magnificent views all the way. The official guide to the Côtes d'Armor declares 'It's a shame that there is no road along the Trieux estuary'. Far from it! Here in the heart of holiday Brittany is a place where the mighty automobile cannot venture, where the splendid views of the estuary and the fine woodland are for walkers alone - or almost alone, since the other way to enjoy them is to take the train.

This area certainly is popular with holidaymakers. Not far away is the Pointe de l'Arcouest and the Île de Bréhat, the port of Paimpol and some fine sandy beaches along a most attractive stretch of coast. But the Bois de Penhoat-Lancerf sweeping down to the estuary of the Trieux is definitely 'off the beaten track' and well worth discovering. Despite their absence from the guide books, these woods are well-managed, with excellent paths and good waymarking - and a regular train service. The views are quite splendid and there is lots of interest along the way.

The walk starts from the Site de Frinaudour, beside the confluence of the Leff and the Trieux. The place is very peaceful and picturesque, the silence broken only by the occasional train crossing the Leff viaduct. The slight widening at the end of the road is hardly a car park - and, as the river here is tidal, take good care where you park your car if the water is low. From Frinaudour the path climbs quite steeply and is soon high above the river with some fine views. Almost opposite, the imposing Château of Roche-Jagu commands the river from a similar height. At Coat Ermit, on the inside of the river bend opposite the château, you come across some old retting tanks - once used for soaking flax to remove the green parts and leave the fibres that make linen. The process produced such a powerful all-pervading smell that the tanks had to be located as remotely as possible from human habitation. A board (in French and English) explains the whole process.

Beyond Coat Ermit, in a clearing in the trees just above the river is the Manoir de Traou Nez - now the Maison de l'Estuaire, owned by the Conservatoire du Littoral and dedicated to the protection of these woods and riverside. As the Manoir de Traou Nez, the old stone house was, in 1923, the scene of a famous murder which has remained unsolved - referred to rather enigmatically as the Seznec affair. The somewhat spooky setting seems one that Agatha Christie might have aspired to. After more climbing, cliffs and woodland, you have a choice - return over the moorland above the estuary or continue to the village of Lancerf and catch the train. If you choose the latter, you can see some 13th century crosses near the roadside and visit the tiny rustic chapel at Lancerf where a son of Napoleon is buried. The moorland route offers easy walking on springy-turfed paths lined by gorse, pines and heather - a pleasant return to the riverside at Frinaudour.

# Directions

**1**. From the estuary at Frinaudour, walk back up the road, pass
under the viaduct, and take the first road on the left, which goes
steeply uphill. Pass the railway halt on your left, and farther on,
take the track on the left, just after the first house. A marker post
directs you to Coat Ermit. This narrow track bears right and
climbs through the trees to reach a broad track at a T-junction.
Turn left here, still following signs to Coat Ermit. Now suddenly
there are fine views across the estuary - you are almost
opposite the castle of Roche-Jagu. The path goes on across
gorse and heather and through woodland of chestnut and

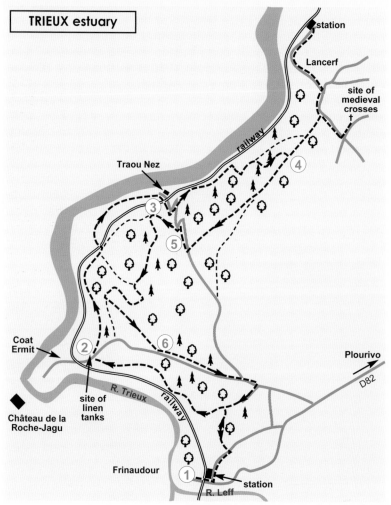

TRIEUX estuary

station
Lancerf
site of medieval crosses †
railway
Traou Nez
④
③
⑤
Coat Ermit
②
site of linen tanks
R. Trieux
railway
⑥
Plourivo
D82
Château de la Roche-Jagu
Frinaudour
①
station
R. Leff

beech. At one point you divert to skirt behind a house, after which the track narrows a little but is still obvious. Eventually you descend to the road at Coat Ermit.

**Château de la Roche-Jagu**

2. Your path continues ahead across the road, and is now signed to Traou Nez. On the left, where the path leaves the road, are the old retting tanks for the flax. Continuing ahead through the woodland, you soon reach a sort of path cross-roads, where you cross straight over. Orange and yellow bands a few metres on down the track confirm you are on the right road. The path again runs through woodland high above the river, and as you pass under the high tension lines, you have another fine view of Roche-Jagu. Descending now to a valley, you come close to the railway line and a path junction. There are now two routes to Traou Nez: take the orange route to the left, which descends to cross the stream at the bottom of the valley. The path then joins the stream to pass through a tunnel under the railway. Continuing ahead on the far side, the waymarks are yellow again. The path goes down to the edge of the river, and follows it to reach the Maison de l'Estuaire at Traou Nez.

3. Now follow the road under the railway, climbing uphill away from the river. At the hairpin bend to the right, take the track on the left, signed to Lancerf. This is magnificent woodland with a preponderance of chestnuts - and, of course, pines. The path reaches a valley and curves inland. Crossing over the stream, it bears left and continues climbing with good views to reach a track junction, where you bear left. This path now wends its way through young pines and heather heading away from the estuary. Soon it arrives at a wide hard-surfaced track.

4a. To complete the circuit to Frinaudour on foot, turn right on the broad track and keep to it for about 350m. Now take a grassy track that leaves on the right, at an angle of about 20° to the main track. In about 800m this grassy track arrives at a road - this is actually the road running down to Traou Nez again. Turn right and keep to the road around two hairpin bends.

**4b**. If you wish to continue to the station at Lancerf, turn left here and keep straight ahead to descend to the road. At the road turn left to Lancerf. (If you wish to see the crosses, turn right instead, and then, in about 100m, left. Both crosses date from around the 13th century, and are thought to be associated with battles against the Normans or the English.) Heading again for the station in Lancerf, keep left in the village following the signs.

**5**. Just after the second bend, take the track on the left. This track climbs uphill into the woods again, and, after about 300m, reaches a track junction. The broader path ahead goes downhill slightly, but you turn sharp left and climb on a track winding through the pines. Waymarks appear as you go, and you follow them across the top of the hill. At the junction under the high-tension lines, you go straight ahead. After the path begins to curve to the right, another junction is reached, and you cross the stream to go straight ahead in the direction of Coat Ermit. The path continues to curve around, but soon you reach another junction, in a clearing. Here take the broad grassy track on the left with banks of pine trees set back on either side. Keep straight ahead on this to join the road to Coat Ermit.

**6**. Turn left on this road (away from Coat Ermit). In about 700m, keep ahead (right) at the road junction. Then take the first road on the right, the Route de Ker Bruc. A waymarking post stands in the hedge opposite. Descending on this road, in about 300m you reach a track on the left - the track you came up earlier at the outset of the walk. The marker post indicates only Coat Ermit (straight ahead), but on the other side of it you will see Frinaudour signed. Turn left down this track and, finally turning right on the road, retrace your steps to the riverside.

**Site de Frinaudour**

## More walks in the area

- It is possible to enjoy an interesting walk along the south bank of the River Leff from the confluence at Frinaudour. Cross the river at the Pont de Houel and continue along the water to the recently restored mill, Moulin de Guézennec. Return along the same route (as there is no other bridge over the river).

- The coastal path GR34 arrives on the east bank of the Trieux having crossed the bridge from Lézardrieux. It then follows the river to the sea and the delightful port of Loquivy - apparently a favourite haunt of Lenin! The GR then skirts the coast to the Point de l'Arcouest - a spectacular journey with wonderful sea views across to the Île de Bréhat. The route then heads south to Paimpol, passing the widows' cross at Pors-Even, where wives of missing fishermen looked hopefully out to sea, and the little chapel at Perros-Hamon where the names of the lost fishermen are written in the church porch.

- The Île de Bréhat is in fact two islands connected by a bridge built by Vauban in the early 18th century. There are many footpaths on the island, but a whole circuit is 15kms with lots to see - chapel, tide-mill, harbours, woods, lighthouses and pink shingle beaches.

## Places of interest nearby

- The Château de la Roche-Jagu is a fine edifice built in the 15th century. Its interior is surprisingly Renaissance - but the most impressive feature is its gardens, including walled gardens, water gardens, camelia woods and foreign gardens. The grounds cover 30 hectares and there are three marked walks.

- The Île de Bréhat is a 15 minute crossing from the Pointe de l'Arcouest. There are no cars on this idyllic island and there is lush Mediterranean vegetation of mimosas, figs and hydrangeas. The sea views are superb in every direction and you can climb a Buchanesque 39 steps to the viewpopint at La Chapelle St-Michel. Cross the bridge to the northern island for greater solitude.

- The Abbaye de Beauport, south of Paimpol, dates from the 13th century and enjoys a splendid setting by the sea. This was once a stopping place on the pilgrimage route to Santiago da Compostela. The abbey is open to visitors all year.

| WALK 16 - Cliffs and coves around the Cap d'ERQUY |||
|---|---|---|
| **Length** 9½kms | **Time** 2½hrs | **Level** Moderate |

**Location & parking:** the port at Erquy. Erquy is on the north coast, about 20km north of Lamballe. The port is at the north end of the town beach. There is parking all along the promenade and in various other sites in the town. It is also possible to start this walk from the car park at the Plage du Guen (Point 2) or the car park on the Cap d'Erquy (just after Point 3).

**Refreshments:** plenty of choice along the sea-front at Erquy.

**Notes:** this is an easy walk (apart from the flights of steps) suitable for trainers, but carry fluids and don't forget the sun cream. Near the end there is a rather adventurous option around the cliffs, which you should not even consider if you have children with you. It does, however, have its rewards. There are safe swimming beaches at Erquy. (Map: IGN Top 25 0916 ET)

## Introduction

The north coastal path of Brittany, the GR34, must be one of the most scenic footpaths in Europe. Here it is at its very best, giving you a magnificent walk along the clifftops, with fine views of the rocky coast and the fishing port of Erquy, famed for its scallops - coquilles Saint-Jacques. You can see them in crates beside the harbour and you can eat them in the many restaurants along the sea front. With a fleet of more than 80 boats, this is a fishing port in the most picturesque of settings - tucked beneath high cliffs and looking out on a perfect horse-shoe bay fringed by pines. It is, of course, popular with holiday-makers, and in July and August can be quite crowded. But there is plenty of space for everyone on the seven beaches of white sand, of which Erquy is justly proud.

Above Erquy is a plateau of land that for the last thirty years has been designated an area of outstanding natural beauty. This is the Cap d'Erquy, where heather, gorse, bracken and pine trees, turquoise sea and white-edged rocks stun you with their perfect combination. And there are distant views: behind you, Cap Fréhel with its lighthouse, and ahead, the wide sweep of the Bay of St-Brieuc leading to the Pointe de l'Arcouest and the Île de Bréhat.

The walk starts from the port and crosses the promontory to reach the coast and the GR34 at the Plage du Guen, a fine sandy beach. Climbing then to the cliffs and the cape, this walk with its truly splendid setting offers lots more of interest before you return. Continuing from the cape, the route passes a little grey stone building that was once part of the coastal defences set up by Louis XVI in the 18th century. Close by and looking out to sea is another little stone building with much more sinister connections. Called a Four à Boulets, it was built around 1794 as a kiln to raise cannon-balls to 'red heat' before firing, in order to set fire to wooden ships. Its primary target was the English fleet. From here, the descent into Erquy on the GR is something of an experience as the path clings to the cliff-face - and it is an experience you may choose to do without! But taking the cliff path will provide you with a unique bird's eye view of the fishing fleet and harbour. It will also take you past Les Lacs Bleus (although they look more brown), which were apparently left after quarrying stone here for the pavements of Paris in the 19th century. A return along the road is a safer alternative, but whatever you choose, Erquy is waiting at the bottom of the hill and you should not miss the coquilles Saint-Jacques.

**The quay at Erquy**

## Directions

**1**. Leave the promenade at the northern end, at the corner with the paved triangle, where the road bears left towards the harbour. Here take the alley, Chemin des Coches, marked with the white on red flashes of the GR. Follow these up some steps to emerge on a wide road. Turn left and shortly bear left off the road following the GR waymarks through some houses and up a steep flight of steps to join another road. Here turn right past the Erquy sign (the GR goes left here) and at the road junction, turn left uphill on the Rue des Grès Rose. You are now on the edge of Tu es Roc with its lovely old houses and have glimpses of sea views on the right hand side. Turn left on the Rue de Pâques (signed le Portuais), and then take the first right - Rue de Tennis. After passing the tennis courts on the left, turn left down the Rue de Portuais. Continue ahead (a road crosses) to the barrier at the bottom. On the far side of the barrier, take the

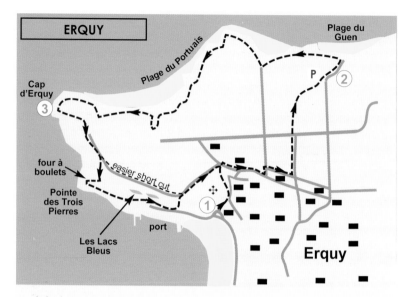

**ERQUY**

Plage du Guen

Plage du Portuais

Cap d'Erquy

③

four à boulets

*easier short cut*

Pointe des Trois Pierres

Les Lacs Bleus

port

P

②

①

Erquy

right hand track leading slightly uphill through the pines to reach the car park at Plage de Guen.

**2**. From the car park, walk through the barriers, heading downhill. At the second small parking area on the left, take the track up the steps, and at the fork of the tracks, bear right. You have now joined the GR34 and can follow its waymarks. As you climb to the cliff-top there are fine views behind you to Cap Fréhel and, much nearer, the island of St-Michel with its little chapel on top. Again you descend, crossing a track to the beach (now the Plage de Portuais), and then, at the next track, turn uphill on a

**Gorse and heather near the Cap d'Erquy**

rather daunting flight of over 100 steps! The good news is that you are spared the last 5 or so - here you turn right on a well-concealed, but waymarked track. This stretch of coast is simply beautiful. The way continues, down valleys and across cliff-tops, well-waymarked at every junction, to reach the tip of the Cap d'Erquy. From this wild promontory there are views in every direction. Close at hand you can see the town of Erquy and the lovely beaches all the way along to the Pointe de Pléneuf at le Val-André. Beyond, the land swings out across the Baie de St-Brieuc to the Île de Bréhat and the northernmost point of Brittany.

3. From the Cap you turn left, and again follow the waymarked path to reach a car park. Continuing along the road, you can see ahead the little grey building that was part of the coastal defence scheme. Just before reaching it, the waymarks of the GR lead you to turn right on a tiny path. This now leads you out to the Pointe des Trois Pierres and its Four à Boulets.

Les lacs bleus

(**Choice**: From this point the path becomes precarious - if you have no head for heights, or have children with you, you may prefer to return to the road and continue that way. The path rejoins the road in about 800m.)

If you have decided to stick with the path, you will find it well-waymarked. At times it is seemingly cut from the cliffside and at one point there is an excellent view of the harbour (you are suspended vertically above it!). The path also passes the 'blue' lakes left after quarrying and eventually emerges on the road. Here you turn right and, skirting behind the château, descend towards the town. Just before the Erquy sign, you will reach the top of the steps you came up earlier, and can retrace your route following the GR waymarks to reach the port and sea-front.

## More walks in the area

- Bus services in both directions from Erquy make linear walks along the superb coastline possible with an easy return.
- Heading west on the coastal path, a walk of 10kms will take you beside several excellent beaches backed by pine woods to the pleasant resort of Pléneuf-Val-André. There is a magnificent sandy beach here, and the most attractive fishing port of Dahouët is 4kms further on.
- Walking in an easterly direction on the GR34, the resort of Sables-d'Or-les-Pins is 13kms ahead. The route passes the little island of St-Michel with its chapel, which can be reached on foot at low tide, and continues across the very attractive estuary of the River Islet.
- The complete circuit of the cape, returning on a disused railway track makes an excellent - if rather long (20 km) - tour of the area.

## Places of interest nearby

- Pléneuf-Val-André, 10 kms west, has one of the finest beaches on the north coast of Brittany. From the Pointe de Pléneuf there are more excellent coastal views, and the GR34 itself continues south of the town as the very pleasant Chemin de la Guette, leading to the charming fishing port of Dahouët. Just off Pléneuf is the Île de Verdelet - an island bird sanctuary, which can be reached on foot at the lowest of tides.
- Les Sables-d'Or-les-Pins is a purpose-built resort - or, it should have been! The golden sand was imported and the fine residences to attract the wealthy from the cities were built at the end of the 19th century. Unfortunately war intervened, much money was lost and it was never completed. Nevertheless, it has a most attractive beach fringed by pines and is popular for water-sports.
- The Château de Bien-Assis, inland between Erquy and Pléneuf, was built of pink Erquy sandstone around the 16th century and you can visit an assortment of rooms and the French gardens.
- Cap Fréhel is 15kms from Sables-d'Or-les-Pins. This windswept and rocky promontory, high above the emerald sea, is a fine view point - and you can climb the lighthouse too! Beware the crowds in summer, but out of season you may even have this elemental place to yourself. The well-preserved Fort la Latte which again bears witness to Vauban's architectural skills, is a little way farther around the coast.

| WALK 17 - In the valley of the river ARGUENON | | |
|---|---|---|
| **Length** 9½kms | **Time** 2½hrs | **Level** Moderate to strenuous |

**Location & parking:** the Château de la Hunaudaye near Plévin, 16 kms east of Lamballe. From Plévin take the D28 towards St-Aubin, and turn where signed to the Château. There is a car park beside the road just past the Château.

**Refreshments:** the farm beside the Château has a crêperie open every day in July and August and at weekends in May, June and September. Near the start of the walk is the Auberge de Bélouze, a 16th century manor with a restaurant (and herb garden).
There are picnic tables beside the viewpoint at Tournemine.

**Notes:** the path through the woodland can be muddy in winter or after summer rain. There are also one or two steep sections, which could be slippery. It is an ideal walk for a hot day as most of the route is in deep shade - but you might like to carry fluid with you as there is no refreshment en route.
(Map: IGN Top 25 1016 ET)

## Introduction

The deep wooded valley of the River Arguenon is a sharp contrast to the otherwise gently rolling countryside of this part of Brittany. This fairly energetic walk through that valley starts from the splendid Château de la Hunaudaye. The five-towered Château has something of a chequered history. Built around 1200, it was destroyed, rebuilt two centuries later, enlarged, burned down by the Republicans in the Revolution and left in ruins. The French government rescued it in 1930 and since then it has been at least partially restored. Now it is quite an imposing sight, complete with moat, drawbridge and towers, standing at the edge of its eponymous forest. In

**Château de la Hunaudaye**

93

**Beside the lake at Tournemine**

summer, flags fly outside and folk in medieval attire can be seen flitting about the grassy banks as they act out everyday life in the 14th century. Out of season the audience is often school children, but July and August bring in the tourists. Whether or not you venture inside, the setting itself is quite photogenic - and just up the road is an excellent crêperie in a lovely old stone farmhouse, just right for the end of the walk.

From the Château the route leads you through pleasant countryside to the banks of the River Arguenon. Here the river has been dammed to provide a water supply and there is now a twisting ribbon lake some ten miles long in a surprisingly deep valley. The forest spills over the steep slopes to the water's edge and creates an attractive scene where, under a canopy of green, wild flowers thrive in the dappled light. The winding path climbs and descends through the woodland, offering views from rocky heights soon followed by close encounters with the reedy shores. At times the path is flanked by dense vegetation and long fronds of climbing plants hang from the trees. You could be forgiven for thinking you were in the African jungle - at least on a hot day. The path continues all the way around the lake - a distance of 35kms or so - but this walk climbs out of the valley beside a bubbling stream and soon returns you to the château.

# Directions

**1**. From the car park, walk down the road with the Château on
your left. At the fork, keep right, towards St-Jean, and take the
first stony track on the right, waymarked yellow and red. This
track climbs gently uphill and soon there are distant views. On
reaching the road, cross straight over (ignore waymarking to
left) towards Bélouze. Descend the hill and take the right fork, in
the direction of Bélouze, picking up once more the yellow on red
waymarks. Still going downhill, the old Auberge is now on your
right. At the bottom of the hill, bear left on the road and continue
along it to the cross-roads, just before le Fougeray. Turn left
here towards Tournemine. The road now descends to a parking
place and picnic spot beside a viewpoint on the lake.

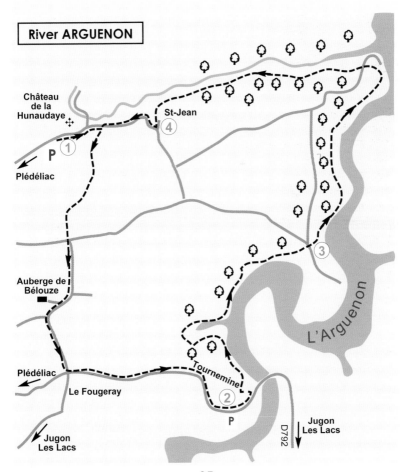

95

2. Just before the road bridge, turn left onto the track beside the water, then immediately left uphill on a grassy track and turn right at the top. Shortly the track descends, and there is a surprise right-hand turn going sharply downhill, waymarked on a tree. Cross over a stream on a plank bridge and climb again on the other side. The roller-coaster path continues, until after a big descent and another stream-crossing, a broad track is reached where you turn right. At the next junction, bear right down beside the water and then bend away from the water following the path uphill and crossing another plank bridge. Continue up the very steep broad track heading away from the river, ignoring the little track along the water's edge. On meeting the track coming in on the left, keep straight ahead, where you will find a waymarked telegraph pole.

3. At the junction with the metalled road, cross straight over (yellow arrow painted on the road) and go straight ahead to where the hard-surfaced road becomes a grassy track. Continue ahead in the woodland, with fine views up an inlet to the east. After a descent, there is a sharp zig-zag climb to reach a grassy track again. Now bearing right on another grassy track (again waymarked), you will find yourself high above the river. The path continues past a danger sign on a steep descent (this is a VTT route) to a sharp left turn at the bottom (missing it would take you straight over the cliff-side!). Once down at the water's edge, follow it around and up the reedy creek to the west. Here keep to the waymarked lower track. Pass the head of the creek and continue over entrant streams to follow beside the main stream of this dense valley. A signpost directs you left to the Château de la Hunaudaye and you continue climbing beside the stream.

4. On reaching the tarmac road, turn right through the attractive hamlet of St-Jean, and follow the road ahead, past the junction, to reach the Château de la Hunaudaye.

## More walks in the area

- There is a footpath all around this lake from Jugon-les-Lacs in the south to the bridge at Plévin in the north - a distance of about 35kms. On this sort of track, the whole journey would take something like 10 hours, but fortunately the circuit can be divided into three loops by the bridges at Tournemine and at Lorgeril. The top loop is then 17kms, the middle just 8kms, and the southern one, 10.5kms - and you can walk the whole route in two or three days.

- For yet another lakeside walk, Jugon-les-Lacs has its own lake to the south of the town. The circuit of this lake is about 16kms but the terrain here is more open and the route passes through several villages.

- If you would like your forest without the lake, there are waymarked paths and circuits in the Forêt de la Hunaudaye. This is rather a dense dark forest, and can be quite muddy in winter. It is closed for 'la chasse' from mid-September to the end of February on Mondays, Thursdays and Saturdays.

## Places of interest nearby

- The Château de la Hunaudaye itself invites you to discover 'the everyday life of a 14th century Breton castle'. The company of actors Compagnie Mac'htiern are to be seen playing their medieval roles every day except Saturday in July and August, and on Sundays and bank holidays in May, June and September. Guided visits are also possible at other times.

- At the village of Saint-Esprit-des-Bois, 2kms west of Tournemine, an ecomuseum known as La Ferme d'Antan is well worth a visit. This faithfully reconstructs the daily life of a farm at the beginning of the 20th century - with plenty of animals, tools of the time, countryside crafts, a forge and even crops now rarely grown (flax, hemp, etc) in the fields.

**Château de la Hunaudaye, open for visitors.**

## WALK 18 - DINAN and the banks of the Rance

| Length 14kms | Time 4½hrs | Level Strenuous |
|---|---|---|

**Location & parking:** the Gothic bridge at the port of Dinan. The port is south-east of the town - follow signs to Lanvallay. Park on the quayside on either bank of the river, or outside the town walls and walk down to the port.

**Refreshments:** restaurant facilities of all kinds in Dinan, port and town. Also bars and restaurants beside the river at le Lyvet.

**Notes:** the first part of the walk includes some fairly steep climbs up banks which can be muddy. Good footwear is needed, along with a certain agility. The east bank is wooded, but the towpath on the west is unshaded - you may need protection from the sun on a hot day. (Map: IGN TOP 25  1116 ET)

## Introduction

North of Dinan, the Rance cuts a surprisingly deep estuary on the last leg of its journey to the sea. Arriving there, it now meets the famous barrage, which makes use of one of the highest rises of tide in the world to produce electric power. Once those tides swept all the way up to Dinan, but when the Ille-et-Rance Canal was created almost 200 years ago, the river was dammed at le Lyvet, and thenceforth Dinan became an inland port. The old buildings along the quayside date from its seafaring days.

The old port at Dinan, the more modern one at le Lyvet, and the wide river between make a fine setting for this classic walk. The first part is fairly energetic, climbing along the high wooded cliffs of the east bank, but you can afford to do justice to a meal at le Lyvet, as the way home is just a gentle stroll along the towpath on the opposite side.

From the riverside, Dinan is to be seen in all its medieval splendour. Clinging to the rocky cliffs high above, the ancient ramparts encircle an imposing jumble of roofs, towers and spires piercing the skyline. Inside the ramparts, the town is just as impressive, with street after street of astonishingly well-preserved buildings from half a millennium ago. In summer those cobbled streets can be thronged with many admirers, but in winter the town goes about its day-to-day business seemingly oblivious of its antiquity, and you can feel you have discovered it for yourself!

From the town, a winding narrow street leads under the ramparts to descend to the port. The old buildings here are garlanded with flowers in summertime and an interesting diversity of craft line the quay. An old 'Gothic' bridge crosses the river and it is from here that the walk starts. The route was originally devised by the Auberge de Jeunesse (Youth Hostel) at Dinan, and so there is an element of adventure about it!

The route follows the right

**The port at Dinan**

bank, taking a detour to cross a marshy swamp that was once a meander of the river, obliterated in the creation of the canal. The steep bank following gives you a first taste of the terrain to come, but your efforts are rewarded by the lovely stone village and superb views at the top. The path then alternately dips to the shore and climbs up the wooded cliffs. On the way you pass a viewpoint known as the Saut à la Puce (Flea's Leap), a château, several villages, a nature reserve and an iron age hill fort. At le Lyvet you return to the river to walk beside the port, where huge sea-going yachts strangely mingle with narrowboats destined for the canal trip south.

The way home along the towpath is easy - no climbs, and not even the excitement of finding the way. Particularly on a Sunday, it may seem that half the population of Dinan along with their grandmothers, dogs and children have decided to join you - not to mention the evidently thriving jogging club and the many oarsmen on the river. But this only adds interest to the walk, and soon the high ramparts of the town appear before you, heralding a return to the quayside.

## Directions

1. Leave the Gothic bridge and walk downstream along the east bank (river on your left). The road ends at the station d'epuration, behind which the path splits into three. Take the centre route between high earthen banks and then bear round to the right beside a field. Continue, skirting the bed of the old river and then cross it on a sort of wooden causeway. The first energetic climb follows, up log steps set in the bank beneath the trees. Turn left at the high wall to reach the road.

2. Here Le Lyvet is signed to the left, a mere 5kms away. Before continuing, cast a glance at the entrance to the Château de

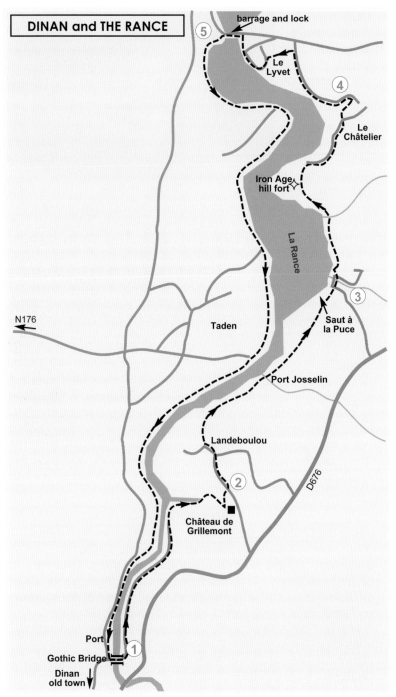

DINAN and THE RANCE

barrage and lock

⑤

Le Lyvet

④

Le Châtelier

Iron Age hill fort

La Rance

N176

Taden

③

Saut à la Puce

Port Josselin

Landeboulou

D676

②

Château de Grillemont

Port

①

Gothic Bridge

Dinan old town

Grillemont a few metres along to the right - you will see its imposing other face across the river as you return. Now continue towards le Lyvet, soon reaching the hamlet of Landeboulou. After passing its château, turn left at a T-junction. Where this road bends left, take the waymarked path on the right. This drops down through woodland to the river and then follows it under the trees. (This part is not exactly a highway and some agility is needed to negotiate the tree roots.) At a little valley, cross the stream on a wooden plank bridge. This is the site of Port Josselin, where in Roman times the river could be forded to reach the village of Taden. Now following the waymarks away from the river, climb a steep bank on log steps. Continuing, you are soon walking high above the river with a field on your right. After 10 minutes or so, a wooden sign marks the Saut à la Puce, where there are fine views down the river. The path descends again quite steeply from here, heading back into the trees and soon reaching a tarmac road.

**View over the Rance**

**3**. Turn left, and immediately right to cross a bridge over the Ruisseau Sainte-Geneviève. Bear left behind the house and, where the track ends beside the riverside reeds, turn right. Crossing some rocks, climb steeply up the bank again. A short climb brings you to a track - follow the yellow waymarks to the left. Continue under the trees, then descend to yet another valley, the Val Orieux. Here cross the stream on a little plank bridge, after which the path bears left, uphill (fortunately well-waymarked). Cross beneath a barrier (a log nailed between trees) and reaching a broad track, keep ahead, still climbing. Shortly, pass signs on the left marking the site of the Éperon Barré, an Iron Age fort in a commanding position high above the river. The deep ditches were part of the rear defences of the fort. Now continue on the broad track, which bears right and then left shortly after to enter the village of le Châtelier.

(**Diversion**: from here there is a fine view of the harbour at Le Lyvet - to see it, take the first road on the left - Chemin de la Cale - and then the first on the right.)

To continue the walk, keep ahead through the village and turn left as the road swings right (Impasse du Val). Shortly, bear right on a cobbled track through a tunnel under the bushes. This leads to yet another little valley, where the stream is crossed on stepping-stones. Another fairly steep climb takes you out of the trees and on to a tarmac road.

**4**. Turn left on the road, from which there are soon fine views. Ahead, the railway bridge spans the curving river, while nearer to you is the port at le Lyvet and beyond it, the barrage. Keep on the road until about 100m before its junction, where you take the waymarked sunken track on the left, leading down between fields to le Lyvet. At its end, turn left on the road to reach the waterside. Now turn right and walk beside the harbour as far as the road bridge, passing a fine assortment of boats and some interesting possibilities for refreshment. At one time you were allowed to cross the barrage itself - you can still see yellow waymarks - but now it is shut off and you must cross the river on the road bridge. At the far side, walk down behind the lock-keeper's house to join the towpath.

**5**. It is now quite simple to find your way home. Continuing on the towpath, at about the half-way point you will pass close to Taden, a village built on an old Gallo-Roman site close to the ford over the river. The riverside here has become a popular picnic spot with tables provided. Display boards tell you that this is a site of special ornithological interest with all manner of winter visitors to this particularly wide stretch of water. In about half an hour after this, you will get that view of the façade of the Château de Grillemont peering down from its rocky height across the water, and shortly after, the ramparts of Dinan loom ahead as you approach the port again.

## More walks in the area

- The other classic walk from the Gothic bridge at Dinan - again popular with the local inhabitants - is along the Rance in the opposite direction, to the village of Léhon with its ancient abbey and ruins of a castle. A short walk of about 3 kms each way, it passes a little island and a lock on the river.

- For a truly excellent walk, you could consider following the GR34C along the west bank of the Rance to Dinard. This is a lot easier than it sounds, as there is a bus service to the villages en route. The whole distance is 40 kms (25 miles), and the route is easy to follow with the usual excellent waymarking of a GR. The views across the estuary are magnificent and on the way you pass several tide mills, many fine beaches and the pretty villages of le Minihic and la Richardais with their harbours. Finally there is the famous power station at the Barrage de la Rance, to which you can make a short (and free) visit.

## Places of interest nearby

- A visit to the old town of Dinan is a must! From the port, walk up the steep Rue du Jerzual and through the arch under the ramparts - this itself is one of the most delightful streets in the town. Alternatively, leave your car in one of the many parking areas outside the walls and enter through a gate - but take note of which one, as the maze of medieval streets within can be quite confusing. Once inside, it is best to wander at will - it is not a town where there are important sites to visit, but it is amazing to find such an array of seemingly perfect medieval buildings. Close to the centre of town is the Tour d'Horloge with its deafening 500-year-old bell. If you have any trouble finding it, just wait for the hour. It is possible to climb to the top of this tower from which there is a magnificent view of the town, the river and surrounding countryside. More excellent views can be had from walking round the ramparts - on the east side of the town, these lead to the Jardin Anglais and the Tour Ste-Cathérine, which looks out over the river and port below.

- The nearby town of Dinard, with its confusingly similar name, offers something totally different. A one-time watering hole of the world's rich and famous who came to enjoy the sea air and mild climate, it retains today many of their exotic residences. Its clientèle, more mixed nowadays, can still take pleasure in the three sandy beaches and subtropical vegetation. In short, it is a most pleasant place to take the family for a day by the sea - but you might also like to visit the curious little Musée du Site Balnéaire, which records scenes from its former life, along with displays on the changing styles of the bathing costume!

- Just south of Dinard is the barrage across the river, and at its centre, the Usine Marémotrice de la Rance. This tidal hydro-electric power station makes use of one of the highest rises of tide in the world (13.5 metres) to generate about 8% of Brittany's energy requirement. You can walk along the dam, be impressed by the swirling currents and take a free tour of the power station.

- The towns of Dinan, Dinard and St-Malo are all seen at their best when approached from the water and in summer there are boat trips on the Rance linking all three.

| WALK 19 - 'Chaos' in the Gorges du CORONG | | |
|---|---|---|
| **Length** 5kms | **Time** 1½hrs | **Level** Moderate |

**Location & parking:** Menhir de Quélénec, which stands just south of the D20, about 16kms east of Carhaix-Plouguer and about 5kms east of the village of Locarn. There is a small parking area adjacent to the road.

**Refreshments:** none on route, but there is an interesting bar/restaurant, the Relais du Corong, in Locarn.

**Notes:** this is a Sentier de Découverte with its own 'bird of prey' logo (actually a hen harrier) and numbered stopping places. The guide book for the route (French only - available from the Maison du Patrimoine in Locarn) describes the geographical and geological features of the area, and details some of the wildlife. Here we follow the route for its own sake but in reverse order. Trainers are adequate, at least in summer, but non-slip soles are a must for crossing the rocks. (Map: IGN Série Bleue 0717 E)

## Introduction

Although not on the usual tourist trail, this is certainly a land that will appeal to walkers. The region was once covered by forest, but since Roman times much of this has been felled to leave *la lande* - the moorland - a windswept and untamed land of gorse, bracken and heather which has a beauty of its own. Through this plateau the rivers have cut deep, often wooded valleys, with waterfalls and landslides of boulders that rolled down the rocky slopes aeons ago. The gorges of Corong and Toul Goulic are quite spectacular. The Ruisseau de l'Étang de Follezou flows through the Gorges du Corong, hidden by huge rounded boulders, made smooth by wind and rain over millions of years - your way lies across them with the stream out of sight far beneath your feet.

In these lonely rivers the water is pure enough to attract otters - they are very shy creatures and not easily seen, but you could look out for their footprints and droppings by the riverside. You may also see the hen harriers - grey with black wing tips - circling in the skies above the moorland.

It seems that this high plateau also had its attractions for prehistoric man - the walk starts from the Menhir de Quélénec, which looks out over a wild moorland valley. The site is very picturesque and there are picnic tables and a display board. From here, the path to the gorge crosses an attractive plantation of pines before dipping to the river. When you first meet it, the

Follezou is flowing quietly enough through the trees, but soon it is tumbling and cascading beside you in a very energetic fashion, before completely disappearing under a huge pile of rounded polished boulders, filling the whole valley - truly a 'chaos'! The Breton interpretation of this scene is that a passing giant emptied the gravel from his shoe here - but another explanation is that the rocky sides of this valley are fissured, allowing rain water to seep in and split off huge fragments, which then become rounded by erosion. The route actually crosses these boulders - and for this you need to be reasonably agile - before climbing out of the gorge through the woods. The way back lies along the edge of the Landes de Locarn, now protected moorland with rare plant and bird life. If you want to learn more about it before you set out, visit the Maison du Patrimoine in Locarn.

**'Chaos' in the Gorges du Corong**

## Directions

1. With the parking for the menhir behind you, cross the road and take the broad grassy track almost opposite. Soon you are walking between plantations of Norway Spruce with the open moorland on the horizon. The path bends left, and you are in wild country with gorse to the left and woods to the right. Rushing water can be heard ahead, and the path turns into the woods to cross the river at the site of a former water-mill. On the far side of the river, bear left and follow the blue flashes on the path through the trees.

**2**. On reaching the tarmac road, turn left, and then shortly, below the parking area, bear right, following the waymarks. Continue ahead, crossing a stream and then following beside a low wall of old stones above the River Follezou, on a most attractive downhill path through the woods. Rocky outcrops loom to the right while the river bounces and skips over cascades of boulders to the left. After a while the whole valley is full of boulders, and the river has disappeared.

Now look out for a blue arrow on a tree directing you to turn left across this rocky chaos (ignore blue markers on the path that continues beside the river).

**3**. Clamber across the boulders to reach a path on the far side that climbs uphill through the trees. This woodland was once the home of charcoal burners and their families. Traces of their slow-burning stacks still remain in the undergrowth. After about 100m, at the cross-tracks, turn right and continue to follow the blue flashes on a twisting path up the side of the valley. Emerging on a sunken lane, turn left and keep ahead to meet a stony road at a car park.

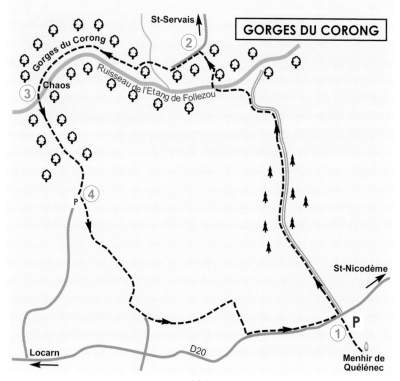

The high moorland - *la lande*

**4**. The high moorland is now before you, but you turn right and follow the fence along the edge of it. The path descends a little and then climbs with increasingly fine distant views as you go. At the height you can see the Monts d'Arrée to the west (and the chapel on the top of Ménez-Mikel - see Walk 24) and, south of these hills, the Montagnes Noires. The path goes on to pass another menhir and then runs along the side of sand quarries where swallows nest in summer. On reaching the road, turn left and continue along it for about 300m to return to the Menhir de Quélénec.

## More walks in the area

- There are several other 'gorge-walks' in the area. The nearest is a short walk in the Gorges de Toul Goulic, a few kilometres away to the east, off the D87 between the villages of Trémargat and Lanrivain. Here the River Blavet disappears to an underground chasm beneath the boulders – quite spectacular!
- Farther to the east are the Gorges du Daoulas (see Walk 13) and still farther east (approx. 45kms from the Corong) are the Gorges de Poulancre. A waymarked walk from the pretty floral village of Saint-Gilles-Vieux-Marché takes you through them. And for yet another 'chaos' in a wooded valley, head for Rostrenen, where the TO should be able to give you details of La Boucle de Restouarc'h. Along with the pretty valley of the

Doré, this walk offers some interesting villages, an old railway track and the fine chapel at Locmaria.

- For a valley walk with something a little different, you are only about 12kms from a short (4.5kms) waymarked walk taking you past the remains of an old Roman aqueduct. The walk starts from Roscoat (head for Locarn, Maël-Carhaix and then Kerogiou where you turn left) and features a stream and water-mills along with the vestiges of the aqueduct, which are identified by green boards. Follow the yellow waymarks uphill from the road junction at Roscoat, turning right across the field at the top of the incline.

- And finally, for something a little educational as well, there is a waymarked 4km circuit from le Moustoir (north of the N164 just east of Carhaix-Plouguer). This is a very pretty short walk, again through a wooded valley, where trees and plants have been named – in both French and Breton. There are also several attractive picnic sites on the walk.

## Places of interest nearby

- The Nantes-Brest Canal is about 20 kms away, just south of the N164. Off that road at la Pie, there is a picnic site beside the canal, which was built by Napoleon as an inland cut for his fleet, thus avoiding the incursions of the British at sea. Since the damming of the River Blavet in the 1920s, the centre portion of the canal between Carhaix-Plouguer and Pontivy is now navigable by nothing greater than a canoe! But its towpath makes a good walk, and from la Pie you can walk east towards Glomel, passing several disused locks along a peaceful reed-fringed stretch of waterway.

- Carhaix-Plouguer itself, though a major crossroads in Roman times, is now not a town of very great note. The TO is housed in the town's most remarkable building, the Maison de Sénéchal, with carved figures and statuettes adorning its 16th century façade. The statue in the square is of a soldier with the grand name of Théophile-Malo Corret, la Tour d'Auvergne. He managed a distinguished career in the Napoleonic army together with studies and publications on the celtic languages.

- South-west of Carhaix-Plouguer (turn right off the D769 at Port-de-Carhaix – where you can again see the Nantes-Brest Canal) is the Kerbreudeur Calvary, dating from the 15th century and thought to be the oldest in Brittany. For another typically Breton elaborate calvary, continue along this road for 2 kms to the village of St-Hernin, with its fine parish close.

# Finistère

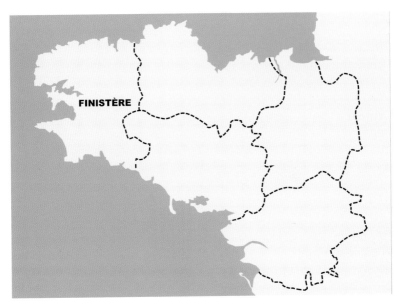

Anse de Penfoul, near Porspoder

## WALK 20 - The enchanted forest of HUELGOAT

| Length 14kms | Time 4hrs | Level Moderate |
|---|---|---|

**Location & parking:** lakeside car park at Huelgoat. Huelgoat lies just off the D764, 35kms south of Morlaix and 15kms north of Carhaix-Plouguer. The lake is on the western side of the town and easy to find. There are parking spaces all along the promenade but if you have difficulty, park in the town.

**Refreshments:** there is a good variety of restaurants, bars and cafés in Huelgoat. On route, there is a crêperie near the Mare aux Sangliers (between points 4 and 5 on the map).

**Notes:** walking boots preferable except in dry weather in summer. The climb up to Arthur's Camp is exposed, otherwise most of the route is in the shade but take water with you. Short cuts can reduce the length of the walk by up to 5kms. (Map: IGN Série Bleue 0617 E)

## Introduction

Beside the town of Huelgoat, in the ancient forest that is part of the Armorican Regional Park, the valley of the River Argent holds an amazing assortment of caves, pools, waterfalls and rock formations. For added measure, this walk follows an old canal to reach a silver mine deep in the forest and climbs to a celtic hill fort with magnificent views. This has to be inland Brittany's top walk - the only possible drawback is that in summer you may find you have rather more friends than you had bargained for to share your path.

Before the arrival of the Romans, all central Brittany was covered with forest such as this - now only Huelgoat and a handful of other places remain. It is a forest of oak and beech, here covering granite slopes and deep valleys where rocks have been eroded over thousands of years to produce weird shapes and strange formations. These are the 'sites', and each has been given an imaginative, if rather fanciful name. The Grotte du Diable, Roche Tremblante and Ménage de la Vierge are all within easy reach of the town.

Farther afield the walk visits more named sites, some beautiful, some spectacular. Le Gouffre is a chasm where the river disappears into an underground waterfall and below it is the Mare aux Fées - a delightful fairy pool. Farther on is the Mare aux Sangliers (Wild Boar Pool - yes, there are those in the forest!) and the Arthurian legends, too, make their appearance with the Grotte d'Artus and Camp d'Artus.

The walk first sets out along the bank of a narrow canal that winds its way through the woodland for some 3kms. It is one of two canals that were constructed in the 18th century to service a lead and silver mine, which was previously known to the Romans. The canal water not only washed the ore but also provided power for the engines. The path beside the canal is very attractive (try it in autumn colours), but there is so much to see later on this walk you may want to take advantage of a short cut that halves the distance. Arriving at the mine, you can still see its entrances and various old buildings - a display board points out the features.

Beyond the mine the route takes an incredibly beautiful path beside the River Argent, passing the pretty Mare aux Fées and climbing to the spectacular Gouffre. Further on, a delightful horse-shoe path (Fer à Cheval) takes you high above the river before you continue climbing past the Mare aux Sangliers to the Cave and Camp of Arthur. Despite these legendary connections, the excavations of Sir Mortimer Wheeler in the 1930s proved it to be the site of a gaulish camp, later taken over by the Romans to house their legions. There are commanding views of the surrounding countryside.

Returning to the rocky valley of the Argent, it is time to test the 100-tonne Roche Tremblante. Apparently it rocks gently when given just a slight push - but you have to find the right spot to apply the pressure. Just before you emerge in the town you can make a descent into the Grotte du Diable on an iron ladder. The story is that a revolutionary soldier, pursued by the Chouans (the army of the Breton aristocracy), hid in this cave and lit a fire to keep himself warm. The pursuing army, seeing a man with a pitchfork in a red glow, thought they had come across the devil himself!

The walk reaches the town beside the Moulin du Chaos, an old mill above a waterfall and rocky gorge with huge boulders in its bed. The mill now houses the tourist office.

**Beside the canal through the woods**

111

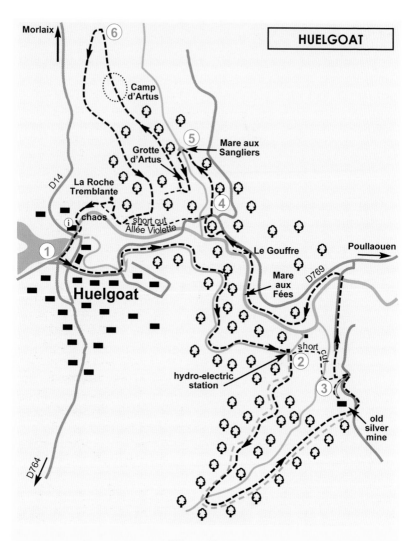

## Directions

**1**. Leave the lakeside promenade by the main road at its centre, the Rue du Général de Gaulle. Passing the town square on the left continue along this road to the edge of the town. After a sharp left bend, signs for Promenade du Canal and Site de la Mine point you off to the right. This level path keeps to the left bank of the narrow canal as it winds and twists through beautiful woodland until suddenly you come upon the little building of the hydro-electric station, where you cross over the canal on a metal bridge.

> **short cut:** Round the back of the building, take the path on the left heading straight downhill, across a little clearing and over the bed of the older second canal. Now bear right following the yellow arrow on the tree and gain a wider downhill path, which emerges from the woods on a bare plateau. Bear right to cross the river on a little log bridge and reach the display board (Point 3). The mine buildings are up the track beyond.

2. Continuing on the canalside path, bear right following the yellow flashed signs to L'Ancienne Mine. Follow the empty canal to the head of the valley, where the entrant stream is crossed on a little bridge. A further 15 minutes walk brings you to the top of the mine beside a gallery entrance. Continue ahead to the broad stony road and turn left downhill. At the junction, turn sharp left, heading for the buildings of the mine and water-wheel. Return to the junction and continue left downhill. At the bottom on the left is the display board.

3. Leave along the broad stony access road with the stream bed on your left and continue to the bridge. On the far side of the bridge, turn left by the wooden signpost (GR 37 to Huelgoat). The path climbs into the woods and soon follows the banks of the river to reach the Mare aux Fées. Climbing more steeply, you arrive at the Gouffre, where the river falls through 8 metres and disappears under blocks of granite. (Here you have the option of climbing to the Belvédère, a viewpoint high on the rock.) From the Gouffre, steps lead up to the road. Turn left along it, and in about 200m, take the path on the left marked Fer à Cheval. This pretty horseshoe path returns you to the road on the other side of the sharp corner.

**La Mare aux Fées**

**short cut:** Regaining the road from the horseshoe path, turn left and continue for 100m to the left bend just before the Pont-Rouge. From here, the attractive Allée Violette continues into the woods on the right of the river. About 300m along, the Stèle des Fusillés high on the bank on the right marks the place of execution of resistance fighters in 1944. At the end of this path you pass the Ménage de la Vierge (where the rocks are supposed to look like cooking utensils) and bear right to reach La Roche Tremblante behind the crêperie. From here follow the yellow flashes to visit the other sites and return to the lake - if you have difficulties, see Point 6.

**4**. Cross the road diagonally to the right to the car parking area. From here take the Sentier du Clair Ruisseau. After about 400m, a sign points to a crêperie on the right but almost immediately, another directs

**La Mare aux Sangliers**

you left to the Mare aux Sangliers. At the bottom of the steps is a little pool with huge rounded boulders and a wooden bridge crossing the water. Continuing over the pool, you climb to a hard track.

**5**. Turn left on this track and pass the cave called Grotte d'Artus on the right. Soon afterwards, take the track on the right signed Camp d'Artus. Follow this round to the right, ignoring the Sentier des Amoureux on the left. The track climbs quite steeply with viewpoints on the right before you enter the camp between two huge granite boulders. On the far side a display board describes its features.

**6**. Continuing downhill to the barrier, turn left following the yellow waymarks on the Sentier du Louarn. This picturesque path winds through gorse and bracken and round rocks on the side of the hill. After about 10 minutes, you come to a path cross-roads. Here turn right, downhill, heading for La Roche Tremblante. At a fork with a waymarked rock, keep left and continue downhill beside a low wall to reach a stream. Now bear right, up to the huge rock on the hill - La Roche Tremblante at last! When you are satisfied you can't move it, continue up the stone steps in the rock behind and follow the yellow flashes to the left, then left downhill beside a rock-face with a big cave (turn left here to reach the Ménage de la Vierge). Cross over the chaos of rocks in the river bed and bear right to reach the Grotte du Diable. From here, continue through a rocky passage to emerge beside the Moulin du Chaos and the lake beyond.

## More walks in the area

- Various walking circuits criss-cross the forest near Huelgoat: the TO by the lake has details.

- There are two way-marked circuits in the forest starting at Locmaria-Berrien, 6kms to the east. The Circuit des Deux Vallées (10kms) follows the River Argent on its way to join the Aulne. A longer circuit of 14kms includes pretty hamlets and the old Roman road from Carhaix to Morlaix.

## Places of interest nearby

- From the viewpoint of La Roche Cintrée to the south of the town you can see across to the Monts d'Arrée.

- The Menhir de Kerampeulven near Huelgoat (just off the road to Berrien), is a fine standing stone with engravings of animals (which probably post-date the stone itself).

- The Monts d'Arrée – the highest 'mountains' in Brittany. From Roc'h Trévézel, you can see all north-west Brittany: Roscoff to the north, Brest to the west and the Montagnes Noires in the south.

- Mont St-Michel de Brasparts (Ménez Mikel). This mountain overlooks the eerie peatbog of the Yeun Elez, the dark reservoir of St-Michel and the nuclear power station!

- Parish closes (les enclos paroissiaux) are a distinctive feature of this area. Most date from the 16th century, with church, ossuary, calvary and cemetery giving scope for intricate stonework and carvings. St-Thegonnec, Guimiliau and Lampaul-Guimiliau are some of the best examples.

- The Armorican Regional Park has good eco-museums such as the Moulins de Kerouat near Commana and the Maison Cornec at St-Rivoal.

# WALK 21 - With the painters of PONT-AVEN

| Length 11kms | Time 3hrs | Level Easy |
|---|---|---|

**Location & parking:** the port at Pont-Aven, at the head of an estuary on the south coast, mid-way between Quimper and Lorient. From the main bridge in the town, follow the road along the west bank of the river to the port (well-sign-posted), where there is plenty of parking – but spaces may be at a premium in high season. Other sign-posted car-parks are available.

**Refreshments:** many bars and eating houses of all kinds in Pont-Aven. Refreshment also on route at the little village of Nizon.

**Notes:** trainers fine in summer, but out of season you may need boots on the woodland sections. After Nizon you can choose to return directly to Pont-Aven, saving about 3kms or 1hr.
The longer walk includes the picturesque banks of the estuary.
(Map: IGN Top 25 0620 ET)

## Introduction

For over 150 years the colourful little town of Pont-Aven has attracted artists from all over the world - the most famous of them all, Paul Gauguin. On this walk there is the excitement of visiting the scenes that inspired some of his paintings, followed by a return along the wooded banks of the winding River Aven, one of the prettiest rivers in Brittany.

It was in 1886 that Paul Gauguin arrived in Pont-Aven. Artists had been there before him and artists are still there today, but his brief stay of three years was enough to ensure a place in history and a never-ending stream of visitors for this little fishing port. It was here that Gauguin and his friend Émile Bernard evolved their new and entirely original form of painting now known as synthetism, a style that rejected conventional perspective, surrounding vivid blocks of strong colour with thick and heavy lines. It was a style as suited to the landscapes and religious themes of Brittany as it was, later, to the islands of the South Seas.

Gauguin and his colleagues lived near the bridge, in a lodging house that is now a newsagents shop - there is a plaque on the wall. You can still appreciate the scene that drew them here. Pont-Aven was a town of fourteen water-mills, most of them still around in various states of repair, gracing the banks of the rushing, tumbling, rock-strewn river. Almost magically, that river opens into a wide calm estuary and an attractive port, which in Gauguin's time busied itself with transhipment of corn for the mills. Now pleasure craft alone use the port but the prospect is still a pleasing one. Below the port, woods crowd to the water's edge along both sides of the estuary, and the return path is delightful.

**Port at Pont-Aven**

At the start of the walk, the Bois d'Amour, a most attractive beech wood beside the river above the town, provides your first encounter with the Pont-Aven school of synthetists. Gauguin here taught his pupil Paul Sérusier, and the painting produced that day, on the lid of a cigar box, has become famous as 'The Talisman'. The little house you pass in the woods is the Moulin Neuf seen in that painting. Climbing out of the trees to the hill above, you next come upon Gauguin at the strange, lop-sided, grey stone Chapelle de Trémalo. Inside is a 17th century yellow wooden calvary, which was the inspiration for his 'Christ Jaune', a painting now, like so many others, housed across the Atlantic. Sunken tree-lined lanes lead you on to the village of Nizon where another calvary, a classically Breton one outside in the square, provided the inspiration for Gauguin's 'Christ Vert'. But if you want to see more recent craftsmanship, try to get inside the church here. The stained glass windows by Guével are truly of the most glorious colours and well worth a pause on your journey.

After Nizon, the route passes the obviously haunted ruins of the 15th century Château de Rustéphan, concealed in the woods. It too, was the subject of a painting, this time by Émile Bernard. Artists are then left behind as you head for the estuary to follow the GR along its shores, meandering along the rocky, tree-lined banks with views of boats and water.

## Direction

1. Walk from the port towards the bridge in the centre of the town, passing water-mills on both sides of the river, one of them converted to a first-class restaurant. Do not cross the bridge, but continue ahead up the Rue Émile Bernard (noting the little Gothic-style loo on the river bank). Take the first turning on the

right - the Promenade Xavier Graal. This flower-bedecked path on an island in the river is dedicated to a native poet and journalist. Once over the footbridge to the island, turn left, then left again, crossing another footbridge to leave the island and reach a road. Turn right and continue uphill almost to the top, then follow a sign on the right to the Bois d'Amour. Cross under the bridge to emerge in splendid beech woods with rocks cascading to the river.

2. Keep to the broad path beside the river for about 800m, passing a small grey stone cottage, the 'Moulin Neuf' of the Talisman painting. On reaching the tarmac road, turn left towards the trout farm and, almost immediately, left again up the hill on a track,

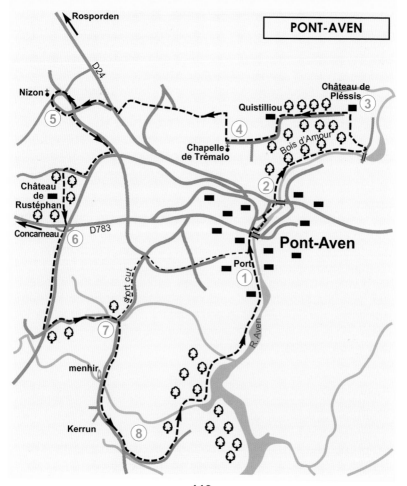

once more in the woods. Near the top of the hill at a clear junction, leave the Bois d'Amour circuit, turning right along a track lined by tall trees, to the gates of the Château du Pléssis.

**3**. Here turn left into an avenue that ends at the farm of Quistilliou. Here follow the road around to the left, and straight ahead at the junction, to reach the Chapelle de Trémalo. The little chapel is usually open and you can admire the old beams and carvings of the interior as well as the calvary that was the model for Gauguin's painting.

**4**. Just past the chapel, take the tree-lined track to the right (signed Ste-Maude). This bears left at the top into another broad track beside woods. Cross a small road and keep straight ahead into a shady alley between earth banks. Cross another road, again keeping ahead on a sunken track. After passing a farm on the left you reach the D24. Here turn right and, in about 30m, left on a metalled road that leads into Nizon. Passing a lavoir (still in use) you arrive at a car park in a square. Now double back to the right on a small road that climbs behind some fine old oak trees, and at the T-junction, turn left to reach the church with its ornate calvary that was Gauguin's inspiration. If the church is locked, it should be possible to obtain the key - those windows are magnificent from the inside only!

**5**. Leave the church on the Rue des Grands Chênes and again reach the car park in the square. Keep this on your left and continue ahead for about 400m to a cross-roads. Turn right, and after another 400m, turn right again, signed to Rustéphan. Just before the farm buildings, take the track into the woods on the left. The ivy-clad remains of the Château de Rustéphan peer eerily through the trees on your right. Continue ahead on the

**Château de Rustéphan**

woodland track and you will soon find yourself walking beside an old wall between trees that once lined the drive to the château. On reaching the tarmac road, turn right for 20m to reach the main D783.

**6**. Cross straight over to take the road opposite, which leaves through a lay-by with picnic tables and toilets (signed Kernonen). Keep on this road for about 800m, then at a cross-roads, turn left on a quiet pleasant road beside and through woodland. After about 500m, a larger road is reached and you have a choice.

---

**short cut:** Turn left on the road, and follow it for about 800m. At a cross-roads in a village, turn right on a grassy and stony track running past houses for about 400m. At the tarmac road, cross straight over and go ahead down another rough road. At its end, a grey stone wall faces you and there are tracks left, right and centre. Take the grassy track ahead and follow it downhill as it bends and winds, goes down steps and finally emerges on a tarmac road which comes out on the promenade near the bridge. Turn right to reach the port.

---

**7**. To continue with the main walk, turn right and walk along the grassy verge for about 800m to a road junction in the village of Kerrun. (On the way, after a left-hand bend, look right to see a huge menhir beside the road.) At the junction, bear left, and at the next junction (20m), keep straight ahead (ignore signs to Kerrun here). Continuing downhill for about 300m, just after the road bends right, you will see a stone arch on the left where a broad track leaves the road.

**8**. Turn left here (signed Kerscaff Tal-Moor) and follow the gravelly track with stream on the right to reach a fork. Keep left here, away from the houses (ignore the GR waymarks to the right). In about 150m, at a junction, with a stone wall ahead, bear left following GR waymarks on a tree. The path goes through an alley between the trees, at the bottom of which you cross over a wall and continue on a path through the woods. After a while (and some stone steps) you will pick up a Sentier Côtier sign and more GR marks. The way back is now easy to follow, an attractive path winding through the trees beside the estuary. All too soon you reach a car park, and from there continue on the road beside the estuary, still with fine views, to reach the port at Pont-Aven.

# More walks in the area

- The well-waymarked GR34 follows the attractive west bank of the Aven to reach the sea at Port Manec'h - a distance of about 13kms, which will take you about 3½ hours. Unfortunately there is no bus service, so you will need a taxi to return.

- For a shorter walk, you could park in the woodland car park just past the sea mill at Hénant and follow the GR along the west bank as far as Kerdruc (4 kms), a most picturesque little port with a couple of bar/restaurants to provide you with lunch.

- Farther afield, the GR34 follows the coast to the west and east of the Aven estuary. To the west are cliffs and fine beaches, including Raguénez Plage with its island, while to the east, beyond the estuary of the Bélon, the coast is more rugged with cliffs, coves and fishing villages.

# Places of interest nearby

- Pont-Aven itself is full of interest - although it unfortunately may be rather crowded in summer. Artists' galleries and exhibitions are everywhere, and the town's Musée is worth a visit. There are plenty of paintings from the Pont-Aven school, but disappointingly, Gauguin himself is represented by only a couple of canvasses which do not seem to bear much relation to the splendours of his work to come.

- Going farther away, the little ports of Kerdruc and Port Manec'h on the estuary of the Aven are each delightful - they are mentioned above in the More walks section. Farther east, the tiny port of Brigneau on its own estuary is interesting, and here you can see a few of the old thatched cottages (chaumières).

- Kerascoët and Kercanic, two villages to the south-west of Pont-Aven, are well preserved as 'villages typiques'. Here again are the thatched houses, but (particularly in Kerascoët) you can also see the 'pierres debout' - huge granite stones more than 2m high - of which the houses of three or four hundred years ago were constructed in this area.

- If you have worked up an interest in Gauguin, you could pursue him to the seaside town of le Pouldu (south-east), to which he retreated after Pont-Aven. Here he lived at an inn that is now the Café de la Plage and achieved notoriety by swimming naked in the sea. As usual he was penniless and left le Pouldu for the South Seas paying his landlady with only a few paintings left behind! These, of course, are now priceless and no longer in le Pouldu - but you can see prints of them at the well-reconstructed Maison Marie Henry.

| **Length** 10kms | **Time** 2½hrs | **Level** Easy |
|---|---|---|

**Location & parking:** the port at Carantec at the start of the causeway to the Île Callot. From Morlaix take the D73 - the coastal road, and much prettier than the much faster D58 you are encouraged to use. From Carantec centre follow signs for the port and Île Callot. Park alongside the port or in the car park nearby.

**Refreshments:** restaurants on route at the port and at Plage du Kélenn; none on Île Callot.

**Notes:** no footwear requirements other than trainers. The route follows the coastal path, with a few gentle climbs and descents and a short section through the town on roads. The two best bathing beaches are also included. If going out to the Île Callot (extra 3kms each way), check the hours of the tides, posted at the end of the causeway. (Map: IGN TOP 25 0615 ET )

## Introduction

Carantec has an enviable position on a hilly peninsula breaking into the heart of the Bay of Morlaix. A century or so ago it was nothing more than a little fishing village, but Parisians spotted its potential as a resort, hotels were built, and Carantec became 'fashionable'. Happily it remained unspoilt and is today a favourite destination for family holidays. Sandy beaches are on all sides, and the views in the bay are in the best traditions of Brittany - cliffs, coves, boats, pines and a myriad of rocky islands in a turquoise sea. The walk here will take you all around the peninsula, passing many of those beaches and a variety of viewpoints, each with its own aspect on the bay.

On the peninsula's western shores where the walk begins, the views are across the estuary of the Penzé to the slender spires of St-Pol-de-Léon, the cathedral and the bell tower of the Kreisker Chapel. Beyond is the port of Roscoff, usually dominated by the vast bulk of the currently docked Brittany Ferry. The route from here crosses the town to the eastern shore, where the views are of the Rade de Morlaix, the estuary of the Morlaix River before it empties into the bay. Farther on, the Pointe de Pen al Lann overlooks some interesting offshore islands. The nearer is the green Île Louët with its little lighthouse, while beyond, the grey bulk of the Château du Taureau seems to rise directly from the sea. The fortress you see today is unmistakably the work of Vauban, but it was built on the site of an earlier defence created by the people of

Morlaix after an English raid in 1522. Morlaix was sacked while its dignitaries were out feasting and they vowed that never again would the town be taken unawares! In recent years the fort has been a prison, a private residence, and a sailing school.

The Pointe de Cosmeur and the Chaise du Curé give views over the more distant islands in the bay, which are now an ornithological reserve. One fine beach succeeds another here, and you may be tempted to stop at the attractive informal restaurants of the Plage du Kélenn.

Either before or after your walk, a visit to the Île Callot is a must, if only for the adventure of crossing the causeway, possible only at low water. In the 6th century the island was a base for marauding Danes, pirates who stashed their ill-gotten gains out here. The local Breton ruler, a Christian, vowed that if he could vanquish the Danes he would build a chapel to Our Lady on the site where the chief Dane had pitched his tent. All went according to plan, and the attractive chapel of Notre Dame de Toute Puissance (Our Lady of all Power) is today a place of pilgrimage. Around the chapel is a village and a farm with typically Breton fields of artichokes. Farther out, the tip of the island is a nature reserve with splendid wild flowers and more excellent views - a pleasant spot to picnic and watch birds and boats going about their business. But don't forget the hour of the tide.

**Islands in the Bay of Morlaix**

# Directions

1. From the end of the causeway, walk along the Rue du Port (with the sea on your right). Where the road turns away left, go down onto the beach, following GR waymarks. Continue along the shore, past the Sibiril monument (Ernest Sibiril was a wartime Resistance fighter who, with his colleague M. Guegen, was responsible for a network which allowed almost 200 allies to escape from occupied France). Cross in front of the Sibiril boatyards and the slipways, take the narrow alley on the left, alongside the wall immediately before the oyster farm.

**2**. At the road, cross directly to the stony track opposite. Climb uphill, with increasingly fine views across the bay behind. At the fork, keep right. The track soon becomes a tarmac road leading to a T-junction. Turn left here and go straight ahead at the roundabout, following signs to Centre Ville. After 200m, bear right at a second roundabout, again follow the Centre Ville signs. After 300m, at a third roundabout, go straight ahead on the Rue François de Kergrist.

**3**. At the end of this road, turn right on the Rue de Tourville, following signs to the Plage de Kélenn. Keep ahead for about 400m (ignoring signs to Plage de Clouët) to yet another roundabout. Here keep straight ahead following signs to Pointe de Cosmeur, and again pick up the GR waymarks. After 100m, these direct you right, into a little road heading downhill to the sea, with fine views of the sandy Plage du Clouët and across the estuary of the Morlaix River to the Pointe de Barnenez.

**4**. At the oyster culture centre, keep straight ahead between the buildings. If you feel unwelcome here, you will soon be reassured - at the end is the Maison de Huitres, where the proprietor will be pleased to sell you some for supper. Continue now behind the building, ignoring the broad uphill track. Follow the waymarks on to the beach, almost

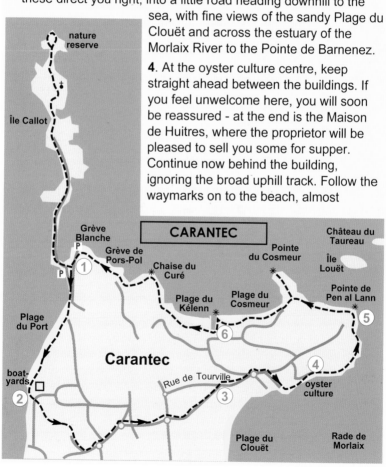

## WALK 23 - Rough seas off PORSPODER

| **Length** 11kms | **Time** 3hrs | **Level** Easy |
|---|---|---|

**Location & parking:** opposite the church at Porspoder. From Ploudalmézeau, take the D168 to Kersaint, and then the D27 south-west to Porspoder.

**Refreshments:** bars / restaurants in Porspoder and at Argenton.

**Notes:** good coastal paths - trainers quite suitable in summer. There is very little shade. Bathing possible at Porspoder and the Anse de Penfoul, but the seas are often more suitable for surfers than swimmers. (Map: IGN TOP 25  0416 ET)

## Introduction

The north-west coast of Finistère is as dramatic, and the seas as turbulent, as one might expect from shores facing the mighty Atlantic. It is also incredibly beautiful. This is the country of the Abers, long tidal estuaries formed when sea levels rose at the end of the Ice Age. Unlike the estuaries of the north coast, these are not fed by major rivers but by tiny streams, and their sides slope less steeply while their beds are less deep. The abers face west, and are at their most beautiful in the evening, when their waters reflect the rays of the setting sun. In day time, a thousand boats bob on the full tide. Between the abers, the coast is rocky and indented, with long bare promontories and off-shore reefs and islands. There are harbours shielding boats from the Atlantic gale, and occasional beaches of glorious white sand.

Perhaps in keeping with the landscape, this is an area rich in prehistory, and particularly in menhirs. There are so many of these that they seem to attract little local attention - the menhir you pass on this walk is all of 7m high, but it stands unmarked in a field where the farmer has carefully ploughed and sown around it. Nearby are two other menhirs of even greater dimensions and many lesser ones are dotted around the countryside.

This walk follows a short section of the coastline between the abers, north of the small town of Porspoder. Before you set off you can choose to walk up to the Pointe de Garchine, where from a high point with an orientation table, you have a view over the whole rugged coast and white-flecked ocean. From here the coastal path, the GR34, leads you on to the island of St-Laurent and around the harbour at Argenton. Further on you can divert to the little chapel of St-Gonvel and the adjacent dolmen beneath a hawthorn tree before walking on beside a long rocky bay.

Contrasting with this are the white sands of the pretty Anse de Penfoul, a bay that attracts surfers at low tide. The return is over high ground, from where you can again view the coast and, across a field, the lonely menhir of Kerhouézel.

**Chapel of St-Gonvel**

# Directions

If you wish to start immediately on the route, take a track behind the church that leads down to the shore. A visit to the orientation table will add about half an hour to your journey.

1. **To the orientation table**. Keep the church on your right and turn left, following signs to GR34 and then Table d'Orientation. Coming to the top of the hill, turn right towards the coast. Leaving the table, turn right down the coastal path. On reaching a hard-surfaced road, follow it for a short distance then leave it on the left again. Passing a lavoir, you soon come close to the church at Porspoder. **Join here if you have not visited the orientation table.** Following the GR waymarks, swing left towards the 'peninsula'. St-Laurent is in fact virtually an island, connected only by a narrow causeway. The path heads for this and crosses it. Turn left around the island. There are views of the Phare du Four out to sea. You may be able to distinguish the ruins of a chapel, a cromlech and a menhir together near the far shore. Afterwards, the path passes an old blockhouse and continues along the north shore and back to the causeway.

2. Now bear left and take a track across the grassland behind the shore. Cross the road going out to the Presqu'île du Vivier and continue ahead, joining a road leading to the port at Argenton. Here, cross into a sandy alley and follow the waymarks to the road alongside the harbour wall. As the road swings left to reach the Centre Nautique, take the Rue des Amiraux on the right. This leads to another track skirting a pretty bay, soon to reach a tarmac road beside a little car park, where you turn left.

3. In about 200m, where the road turns sharp right, the Sentier Côtier leaves the road and continues ahead. If you want to see the dolmen and church of St-Gonvel, continue on the road for about 250m; the dolmen and the church are on the left. Return to resume the coastal path, which now skirts a rocky bay (views of the Île d'Yoc'h, the site of another prehistoric tomb). The coastal path briefly joins a road in St-Gonvel, but then turns left again towards a long digit of rock pointing out to sea. Beyond this is the fine white sand of the Anse de Penfoul (covered by sea at high tide). The path turns inland beside the estuary. Just before reaching the road at its head, you are suddenly directed left across the top of the beach and then on a path under the trees to a car park.

4. Now leaving the GR, keep ahead on the main road. After about 100m, take the small road on the right (yellow waymarks). At

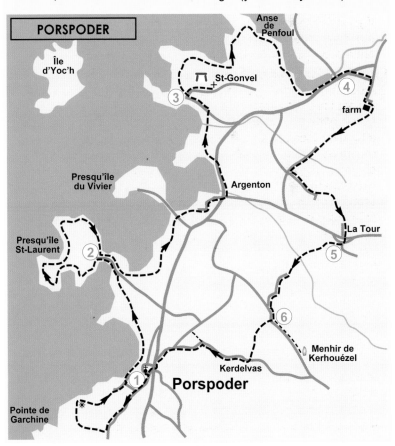

the T-junction, turn right. Coming to a
farm on the left, do not go straight on,
but bear left and, passing the house,
turn right on a track alongside the
hedge. Continue ahead on this track for
800m to reach a tarmac road. Now turn
left, signed la Tour and Château d'Eau.
Where the track forks, bear left to the
main road at la Tour.

**Menhir de Kerhouézel**

5. Cross straight over this road to the lay-
by, and turn right off the road
immediately behind it on a sunken path
that may look a little unlikely - but things
will improve. First though, you must
cross a rather boggy area where a stream descends -the
compensation is the beautiful display of wild flowers. After this
you join a track coming in from the right and continue downhill
on a much improved track to cross the stream. Continuing
ahead, the track reaches a house and becomes hard-surfaced.
After a further 300m or so, at the road junction turn left.

6. In a further 100m, follow the yellow waymarks off to the right.
(To see the menhir, do not turn here, but continue on the road
for about 300m. The huge menhir is in the middle of a field on
your left - but you will have to view it from the hedge. Return to
the waymarked track at the corner.) Continue along the hedge
with good views over the coast. The track meets the road in the
village of Kerdelvas, where you turn right. About 400m along, at
the sharp left bend, ignore the yellow waymarks ahead and
keep to the road. At the 4-way junction, keep left to reach again
the church at Porspoder.

## More walks in the area

- Further north is a circuit of 12kms following a more open
  coastline with higher cliffs. Starting at the chapel of Kersaint
  (see below), it passes the isolated little chapel of St-Samson
  overlooking the rough seas and visits the ruined 14th century
  Château de Trémazan, said to be the landing place of Tristan
  and Isolde in Brittany - and as such has a heart-shaped hole in
  the wall.

- To the south, another interesting circuit is that along the
  northern wooded shore of the beautiful Aber Ildut. The route
  starts from the mouth of the aber at the Rocher du Crapaud

(Toad Rock) and passes Lanildut, a port whose prime export is seaweed.

- If you are interested in menhirs, there are several circuits visiting some of the area's largest specimens. On the short circuit passing Kerloas (9.5m high), you also pass a high viewpoint with picnic benches and an orientation table.

## Places of interest nearby

- If you have not time to walk along the coast north of the Anse de Penfoul, you should at least drive it. There is a fine outlook to sea all the way and you pass the lonely chapel of St-Samson beside the road. There is also a calvary and a fontaine, over to its left.

- Continuing, you come to Trémazan with its view over the Île Verte and the port at Portsall. The road passes the ruined castle associated with the Tristan and Isolde legend and haunted by St-Haude (holding her head in her hands!). Her fate is a sad story, but if you can't meet the ghost in person, you can see her statue in similar posture in the chapel of Kersaint in Landunvez.

- Beyond Trémazan, the road curves past Portsall, and on a headland stands the Dolmen of Guilligui, which, dating from 6000 BC, is one of the oldest in Brittany. Travelling north to Porsguen, you can find in the harbour the anchor of the Amoco Cadiz, the oil tanker that left its horrific legacy to this coast in 1978. Just out to sea is the Île Carn, where there is a huge prehistoric cairn similar to the one at Barnenez.

- Farther on are the abers, Aber Benoit and Aber Wrac'h, both very beautiful, and the rocky shores are guarded by the lighthouse (the tallest in France at 82.5m) on the Île Vierge.

- The menhirs in these parts are remarkable. Kerhouézel was passed on your route, but the biggest menhir of all is just a few kilometres south-east at Kergadiou. This one is fallen, but it is about 11m in length and weighs about 60 tons. Still standing close beside it is a lesser one, a mere 8.8m high.

- South of the D5 from St-Renan to Plouarzel is the menhir of Kerloas. Nicknamed le Bossu (the hump-back), it is 9.5 metres high, the highest standing menhir in France. Its location, its alignment with other menhirs and the distances separating them have been the subject of much discussion and argument. It is certainly possible that the placing of these stones is not random but rather based on mathematical and astrological calculation.

## WALK 24 - Climbing MÉNEZ-MIKEL

| Length 16kms | Time 5hrs | Level Moderate |
|---|---|---|

**Location & parking:** car park at St-Rivoal. St-Rivoal lies 5kms west of the D785 Pleyben - Morlaix road, just north of the village of Brasparts. There is a large car park in the centre of the village, opposite the church.

**Refreshments:** there is a bar/restaurant in St-Rivoal - but none on route.

**Notes:** walking boots required unless the weather has been particularly dry. The climb up Ménez-Mikel is quite gentle - as are later short climbs in the forest. All is on well-defined tracks. After about 10kms you can choose a short (2kms) return by road - but continuing you will have more fine views of the Monts d'Arrée, concluding with a pretty riverside path through the woods.
(Map: IGN Série Bleue 0617 O)

## Introduction

The Monts d'Arrée are the oldest hills in the world, formed in the primary era 600 million years ago, and perhaps originally ten times their height today. They are no longer 'mountains'. Wind and weather have worn the granite down to rounded summits (the Ménez), but within the granite is the harder quartz, and this has remained in places, projecting through in jagged 'teeth'. Such a quartz ridge is Roc'h Trévézel, at 384m the highest point in Brittany. Not far away is Ménez-Mikel, a hill just 4m lower but more conspicuous, its summit marked by a solitary chapel. All around is the wild moorland - wide empty spaces brightened by gorse and heather - barren heights, and valleys filled with woodland. Buzzards circle overhead and you may be lucky enough to glimpse deer - or even wild boar, although these are mostly nocturnal. The Monts d'Arrée have a beauty that is all their own - and, being a part of the Armorican Regional Park, they also boast many waymarked trails.

The walk here starts from the grey granite village of St-Rivoal. After wending your way through the forest you are soon climbing the gentle slopes of Ménez-Mikel - or Mont.St-Michel, to give it its French name. The landscape seems so remote that, approaching the summit, you may feel slightly disconcerted at reaching a road. But the top is still a further burst of climbing away, and unspoilt.

Looking down from Ménez-Mikel, the cloud shadows chase themselves across miles of bare moorland. To the east, often shrouded in its own mist, is the Réservoir de St-Michel (also called Lac de Brennilis), and around it, the desolate peat-bog of Yeun-Elez. Celtic legend has it that this is one of the entrances to hell. Exorcism was practised here in which an

**Church of St-Rivoal**

unwanted evil spirit was passed into a black dog, which was then drowned in the bog. This rather fearful spot was, aptly enough, chosen as the site of a nuclear power station (now being de-commissioned). Turning your back on all this, a ring of summits lies before you - on this side the River Elez has its source, on the other, the River Elorn. On a really clear day, you should be able to see beyond the summits to the sea - the channel coast to the north and the Rade de Brest in the west. Below, your path can be seen heading across the moorland to the forest where you will wander through the woodland with many heights and viewpoints, and an attractive stretch of the GR through the valley of the Rivoal.

## Directions

1. From the car park, take the D42, direction Morlaix. Just past the bar/crêperie, turn right on the road to Bodenna. Walk uphill for about 200m, then take the track on the left (waymarked yellow), continuing uphill through the woods. Reaching the tarmac road, do not step out on it, but rather turn back, and take the broad track to your right. This now descends again through a pleasant area of gorse and pines to reach a road once more.

2. At this road, turn left and walk through the little village of Bodenna. The tarmac now ends, and you continue on a broad earthen track, which bears right and then left, but is well-waymarked. Soon the track climbs out of the woods and you have wider views. Gorse and heather line the path, with pine woods stretching into the distance. The obvious route climbs gently all the way - every track junction waymarked, but essentially you keep straight ahead. Pass under the high tension cables, then keep parallel to them to reach a multiple track junction.

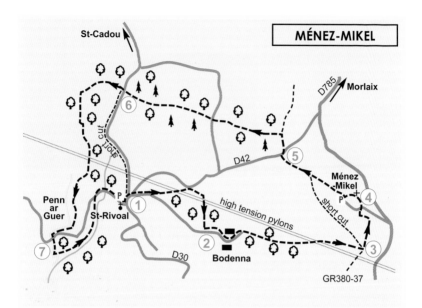

**3**. Take the second track on the left signed to Ménez-Mikel or Mont. St-Michel. (If you should want to avoid further climbing, the first track, Circuit de St-Rivoal, will take you around the foot of the hill to join the route again on the far side.) After a few hundred metres bear left, picking up yellow waymarks again. Coming up below the road, turn right up a narrower track to meet it. A signpost informs you that you are now on the Circuit des Landes et Tourbières (Moors and Peat-bogs). Cross straight over the road and continue climbing to the summit.

**4**. The chapel of St-Michel was built here in the 17th century. Adding its height to that of the hill, the cross on its top is actually the highest point in Brittany. When you are ready to descend, continue downhill heading in the same direction - with your back to Yeun Elez. A flight of wooden steps leads you down to a car park. At the right hand side of this there is a signpost - ignore what it says but follow its direction. The track heads out across the moor vaguely in the direction of the radio transmitters on the horizon. The track skirting the foot of the hill now rejoins you from the left and you continue down to the main road, the D42.

**5**. Turn right on this road, and after about 20m, sharp left, following the sign for the Circuit de St-Rivoal. The path is again lined by pines and gorse, and soon, at a corner with a field ahead, turns abruptly left. Now the sunken track descends steeply to a stream at the bottom of a valley. Crossing a small road keep straight ahead. The path soon becomes narrower and winds through pine woods beneath a hill rising on the right, eventually reaching a main road.

> **short cut:** To return directly to St-Rivoal, turn left here - you will be back in about half an hour.

6. To continue, cross to the track opposite and begin to climb again through the woods. Emerging at the top you have fine open views of summits on the right. At the track junction, go ahead and then to the left, again signed Circuit de St-Rivoal. At a T-junction just before the high tension lines bear left. The path is now quite obvious and well-waymarked as it descends through the woodland. After 25 minutes or so, at a small road bear left. This road soon reaches the hamlet of Pen-ar-Guer.

7. At the main road, cross straight over to the waymarked road opposite. This descends abruptly, and, at a right hand bend, you leave it to turn left on the GR380-37, a very pleasant track through the woods alongside the River Rivoal. Near a

**Ménez-Mikel**

bridge you join a hard-surfaced track and continue beside the river. Shortly, at the main road, turn right to return to St-Rivoal. Look out for the traditional farm, the eco-museum Maison Cornec, on the corner as you come through the village.

## More walks in the area

- There are many marked walking trails in this area. A brave choice might be the Circuit du Yeun around the reservoir (16kms), according to celtic legend a tour around the gates of hell! In fact it is a walk through a fascinating and fragile protected environment - just don't forget to stay on the marked paths.

- If you would prefer a little moorland with the peat-bog, the Circuit des Landes et Tourbières, which you briefly touched on this walk, is a very pleasant route, and includes the summit of Ménez-Kador.

- From nearby Sizun, there is a fine long circuit (19kms) through the valley of the Elorn and around the Lac du Drennec.

**135**

# Places of interest nearby

The Armorican Regional Park has a particular wealth of eco-museums. This may be 'off the beaten track' country, but there is always something to do on a rainy day!

- Since you are in St-Rivoal, you should visit the Maison Cornec for a glimpse of 18th century rural life. The granite farmhouse has an earthen floor and an outside staircase to the hayloft. Living quarters were shared with the animals for heat, while outside in the yard stood the bread ovens. Stables and barns now display tools of the time and nearby is an old orchard of cider apples.

- A few kilometres north, between Commana and Sizun, is one of the most interesting of the eco-museums, the Moulins de Kerouat. Here is a completely restored mill village on the River Stain, the buildings dating from the 17th century onwards. Houses are furnished in their original styles, from the poorest to the most sumptuous, in which lived a one-time Mayor of Commana. One mill is in working order, and amid much clamour and clatter, you can watch the machinery turning the millstones. Barns, outbuildings, stables, lavoir and much more are all there for you to wander around.

- Another of these eco-museums is the Domaine de Ménez Meur, 6kms away to the west. Here you have an exhibition centre relating to the activities of the Armorican Regional Park, a large animal reserve with wolves and wild boar (at least you can see them here, if not on the walk!), the Breton Horse Centre, nature trails, an adventure playground and restaurant facilities - all adding up to a full day's entertainment.

- Lac du Drennec between Sizun and Commana has possibilities for swimming, fishing, boating and refreshments.

- Near Ménez-Mikel is an 18th century farmhouse, the Ferme des Artisans, which has now become a centre of Breton art and craft. Regional products are on sale and demonstrations are arranged during the summer months - although the centre itself is open all year.

- Another outstanding feature of the Monts d'Arrée is the number of most elaborate parish closes - the combination of chapel, cemetery, calvary and ossuary all enclosed by a wall (see Places of interest nearby under Walk 20). It seems that the villages here tried to outdo one another with the capabilities of their stone masons! Nearby Sizun has one of the most attractive examples.

## WALK 25 - CAMARET and the alignments of Lagatjar

| Length 12kms | Time 3hrs | Level Moderate |
|---|---|---|

**Location & parking:** port of Camaret-sur-Mer. The Crozon peninsula lies between the Bay of Douarnenez and the Rade de Brest. From Crozon, take the D8 west to Camaret. There is parking all along the sea-front facing the harbour.

**Refreshments:** many pleasant sea-food restaurants along the sea-front in Camaret.

**Notes:** well-defined coastal paths - trainers would be quite adequate. There is no shade. There are some fine beaches on route, but if swimming, remember there can be strong currents around this coast. Notices advise you of the risks.
(Map: IGN Top 25 0418 ET)

## Introduction

Camaret was for many centuries a port of some importance, hiding behind the Pointe de Toulinguet and tucked away from the prevailing winds. It is a port enclosed by a long 'jetty' on which stands a chapel - and, perhaps not surprisingly, a defensive tower built by Vauban. This spit of land - the Sillon - is quite natural in origin, the tides and wind here causing a build up of rock and pebble that varied with the seasons. It is only recently that the sillon has acquired its covering of cement and tarmac.

Camaret's importance was at its height in the days of sail. The natural protection of its harbour meant that ships would take refuge here from the Atlantic blast or wait in these waters for the gale to abate before venturing into the Irish Sea. The taverns of the town acquired a reputation for being able to 'entertain' sailors during the boring delay. When sail became a thing of the past, the port became a centre of lobster fishing. Now the lobsters too have gone, the port has assumed an air of melancholia, with skeletons of old boats lying sadly on the shingle.

Camaret was the scene of the first attack by submarine - except that it never quite happened. In 1801, Robert Fulton, an American engineer living in France, had invented a submersible wooden craft propelled by oars. Leaking and difficult to navigate, it could stay underwater for only six hours - long enough to fix dynamite to the hull of a ship. The target for the trial was to be an unsuspecting English frigate moored in the bay. The submarine set out, but became confused in its direction. Meanwhile the frigate decided to weigh anchor and sail off into the sunset - quite unaware of its intended fate. The disillusioned inventor never tried out his submarine again, and it was to be more than seventy years before a successful model was perfected.

From Camaret, the walk takes you first to a cliff-top covered with wild flowers, where a Navy Signalling Station overlooks the turbulent seas. It also overlooks the wide sandy bay of Pen-Hat - but this is no place for a swim. Behind the bay, the grassy cliffs slope up to the distinctive stark ruins of the Manoir de Coëcilian. At the turn of the century, Camaret had found favour with artists and writers. One of these was the poet Saint-Pol Roux, who built here a rather strange Greco-Roman style residence. It was destroyed in a terrible night of desecration and pillage by the Nazis in 1940. The manor also overlooks a vast array of megaliths known as the alignments of Lagatjar - Saint-Pol Roux of course wrote about them. 143 stones now are standing here, most of them in obvious lines - but it is known that originally there were many hundreds more.

Beyond the megaliths the walk continues past old blockhouses, one now used as a museum, and climbs to another rocky outcrop, the Pointe de Pen-Hir. Here a monument to the Free French Forces has a view over the sea from the Pointe du Raz and the Île de

**Alignments of Lagatjar**

Sein in the south to the Pointe St-Mathieu and the Île de Ouessant in the north. Below the point itself, the sheer cliffs are a favourite site for rockclimbers - and if you indulge in a little gentle rock-climbing yourself, you can reach the Chambre Verte, a grassy platform in the cliff with a fine view of the Tas de Pois, three huge rocks that look as if they have been cast into the sea by a giant's hand. After all this excitement, it is just an easy walk along the cliffs and inland tracks to return to Camaret. And even if there are few lobsters in the sea now, you can usually find some in the restaurants beside the port.

# Directions

1. Follow the sea-front to the beginning of the sillon. Continuing on the road, you will see a signpost to the Pointe de Toulinguet. Following the GR waymarks, pass through a picnic area and continue to climb, past a little old fort pressed into the cliffside before reaching the Pointe du Grand Gouin with more excellent views. The path from here is well-waymarked - it descends to the road before turning off again to the right to climb to the Pointe de Toulinguet. Rocks, gorse, heather and wild flowers make this a very attractive headland. There are many paths across it, but whichever you choose, you should arrive at the gates of the fort - now a navy signalling station.

2. From the gates, walk across the moorland to the opposite side, where there are fine views of the sandy Anse de Pen-Hat and the ruins of the Manoir de Coëcilian on the hill behind. Follow a rather indistinct path along the edge, which becomes clearer as it descends across the grassland to the bay. Crossing the end of the road, continue to skirt the bay, then choose any of the tracks that climb the grassy slopes to reach the Manoir de Coëcilian at the top. Take the rough road behind the manor to emerge on a tarmac road. On the far side of this are the alignments of Lagatjar, their windswept grassland now sadly encroached upon by houses.

3. Leaving the alignments at the far end of the field, cross the road again and find a track in the scrubland leading along the top of the cliff. Here you will pick up the GR waymarks again, and these lead you past the blockhouse museum, dedicated to the Battle of the Atlantic. The waymarks briefly bring you down to the road but then leave again to skirt the cliff on the way to the Pointe de Pen-Hir. Soon you come to the monument to the Free French Forces. A vast car park not far away accounts for the sudden influx of people. There is a fine view around the coastline. A path to the left of the monument and viewing platform descends and then climbs to the left to reach a grassy ledge, the Chambre Verte.

**Near the Pointe de Toulinguet**

139

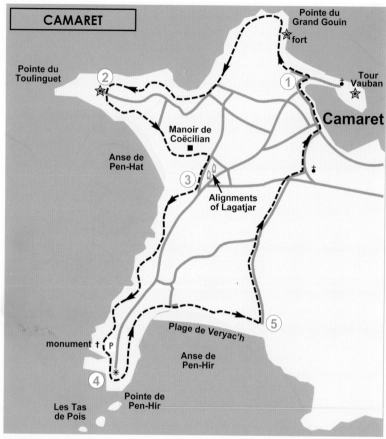

**CAMARET**

Pointe du Grand Gouin

fort

Tour Vauban

Pointe du Toulinguet

Camaret

Manoir de Coëcilian

Anse de Pen-Hat

Alignments of Lagatjar

Plage de Veryac'h

monument †

Anse de Pen-Hir

Pointe de Pen-Hir

Les Tas de Pois

4. Returning to the coastal path, continue around the point to the far side, where a grassy track can be seen sweeping down to another bay, the Anse de Pen-Hir. Reaching the beach (Veryarc'h Plage), you pass a little café and continue along the coastal path again. After a further 15 minutes or so walking, the well-marked path crosses a hard-surfaced road.

5. Ahead the track is signed to Kerloc'h - the continuation of the Tour de Camaret. But on this walk, you turn left and follow the track inland. Coming to the first road junction, keep ahead (slightly right) and at the second junction, keep ahead again on the Rue de Kermeur. This road now descends with good views over the harbour and sillon. At the junction with the main road, take the second road from the right, which leads to the church. Turn left in front of the church and keep straight ahead past the Mairie and the little square to return to the harbour.

## More walks in the area

- The whole Crozon peninsula is contained within the Armorican Regional Park, and nowhere in Brittany is there so much fine cliff walking! The local tourist board have divided the coastal path, the GR 34, into five sections, each of which can easily be completed in a day, ending at a place with overnight accommodation - but you could choose to use a taxi to return to your car each day instead.

- Starting from Morgat (said to be the 'Pearl of the Crozon') there is a 16km circular route entitled De la Baie de l'Océan that gives you a bit of everything, crossing from the high cliffs facing the Baie de Douarnenez to the long sandy Plage de la Palue, looking to the Atlantic. In between is moorland, forest and river valley - a first-class tour of the southern part of the peninsula.

## Places of interest nearby

- The islands of Sein, Molène and Ouessant are visible from the Pointe de Pen-Hir - in fine weather! If you would like to visit them, the company Finist'mer runs trips during high season.

- More boat trips start from Morgat where you can cruise around the rocky Cap de la Chèvre or cross the bay to Douarnenez.

- More popular are the boat trips to the nearby caves at each end of the beach. Scooped out of the multi-coloured rock, these caves are quite spectacular, with 'chimneys' to the cliff-tops high above. Morgat is also blessed with lesser caves, which can be reached on foot at low tide.

- It is well worth heading out to the Cap de la Chèvre just for its superb views. The point (about 6kms from Morgat by road) is occupied by a Naval Station, but you can walk around this to a viewpoint with a telescope. From here you can see all around the Bay of Douarnenez with its beaches and headlands, from the Pointe de Pen-Hir behind you, to Cap Sizun, the Pointe du Raz and the Île de Sein. Walking around the cape, you can see that all the bay is under the watchful eye of Ménez-Hom, looming above the sands of Pentrez-Plage. The view from the summit of this 'mountain' is definitely one of the finest in Brittany - you can't miss Walk 28!

## Introduction

Wild seas and reefs off the Pointe du Raz made it a one-time favourite haunt of wreckers. Now this windswept westerly point is popular with the tourists - but take this walk around the high cliffs and you are likely be facing the elements alone!

The Pointe du Raz is to Brittany what Land's End is to Cornwall. This is the farthest point you can reach, a point where the setting sun sinks far out into the sea. Like Land's End, it attracts its visitors. A centre with shops and refreshments caters for the hordes - but tastefully it is sunken in a hollow and set back from the Point itself. Cars are not allowed past the centre, so to reach the point, visitors must take a walk of around 15 minutes, or catch the navarre, the shuttle bus. To be accurate, the Pointe du Raz is not quite Brittany's most westerly point (that distinction belongs to the Pointe de Corsen beyond Brest), but it does have all the right attributes! The Pointe du Raz is at the very tip of the Cap Sizun, a long triangular finger of land reaching far into the Atlantic below the Bay of Douarnenez.

The Point itself is a high rocky outcrop capped by gorse and heather. Far below, wild foaming seas crash against the dark rocks and all around, the air is full of seagulls blown on the wind. On a clear day, the tiny Île de Sein can be seen squatting low on the horizon. Raz means Race, and it is well-named, for between here and Sein the tide hurries at a great pace and the currents are treacherous. This is a passage much feared by sailors. High on the Point stands the enormous statue of Notre Dame des Naufrages (Our Lady of the Shipwrecks) - an effigy of a half-drowned mariner reaching for the hands of the infant in Our Lady's arms.

The walk sets out from the Point along the southern side. Here you are immediately struck by the prevailing winds from the Atlantic. But the cliffs are bright with gorse and heather and soon you see far below you the tiny Port Bestrée, the high wall shielding a few brave boats from the Atlantic gale. Farther along you follow a wild coast of rocks and reefs before crossing the peninsula. Your first sight of the north side is surprising. Foaming white waves crash on to a wide bay of golden sand. A hotel in delicate pastel shades stands behind. All belies the sinister nature of this spot - this is the Baie des Trépassés, the Bay of the Dead! An explanation for this rather ominous appellation seems to be that with the predominant current, bodies of mariners drowned off the Île de Sein are naturally washed up in this bay. An alternative reason is possibly that, many centuries ago, the bodies of dead druids were ferried from here to their traditional burial place on the Île de Sein. Being Brittany, there are also stories of unidentified boats with lone sailors passing in the night and references to Ankou, the grim reaper! On a sunny day here, you just can't believe it - but visit this spot in a winter storm!

In addition to all this, one of the most famous Breton legends of all time is associated with the lake behind the Baie de Trépassés, the Étang de Laoual. It is a legend with perhaps just a small grain of truth in it. In the 6th century, the Breton capital was the beautiful island city of Ys. The island was low-lying, and the city was protected from the sea by huge gates which were kept locked - King Gradlon himself kept the key. He had a daughter, Dahut, and she fell in love with a handsome young man - who turned out to be the devil in disguise. The devil persuaded Dahut to bring him the key to the sea gates, which he then opened. The sea rushed in, Gradlon pulled Dahut on to his horse and fled before the torrent.

**Near the Pointe du Raz**

143

A voice told him to drop his wicked daughter into the sea to ensure his escape and that of his people. Dahut thence became a mermaid, haunting the oceans and luring sailors to their doom, while Gradlon established his new capital in the town of Quimper. Ys remains covered by the waves. Bretons have no doubt about the existence of Ys - and there is actually some evidence. The only problem is where. The most popular supposition is in the Bay of Douarnenez, but other contended spots are here in the Baie des Trépassés, off the Pointe de Penmarc'h and in the Bay of Erquy.

As you descend the road to the bay, you can contemplate what lies beneath the waters of the lake. But when you turn to go home, you will need to keep your eyes firmly on the ground as the path gets trickier as you go. When you finally round a headland where the cliff ahead seems impossible, you are suddenly spared further difficulties as the path turns inland. In a few minutes you are looking across the heather to the sémaphore and statue on the headland, a scene teeming with people once more.

## Directions

1. Leaving the car park, cross to the information bureau at the end of the line of shops. Behind it is the bus stop for the shuttle and the start of the path out to the Point itself. After about 10 minutes walking on the well-used path, you reach the signal station and the statue of Notre Dame des Naufrages. The rocky tip is still ahead of you - explore it now or at the end of the walk. To follow the walk, bear left (sea on right) on a wide track across the cliff top. After a few minutes the track forks. Take the narrow right-hand path, signed Sentier Côtier. This heads off along the side of the cliff with spectacular views all the way. The path is quite obvious until you reach a fork with a tarmac road ahead. The right-hand path now goes down to Port Bestrée and it is well-worth taking a look down there. The left-hand path continues to meet the road to the port.

2. Whether or not you went down to the port, you will arrive at the point at which the coastal path crosses this road. From here, continue on the coastal path again, following the waymarks. There is a fine view ahead and the path soon passes an arch through the rock as it winds around to a little cove. At this cove, do not take the path ahead, but continue on the coastal path, which climbs again. The coastal path soon passes a pebbly

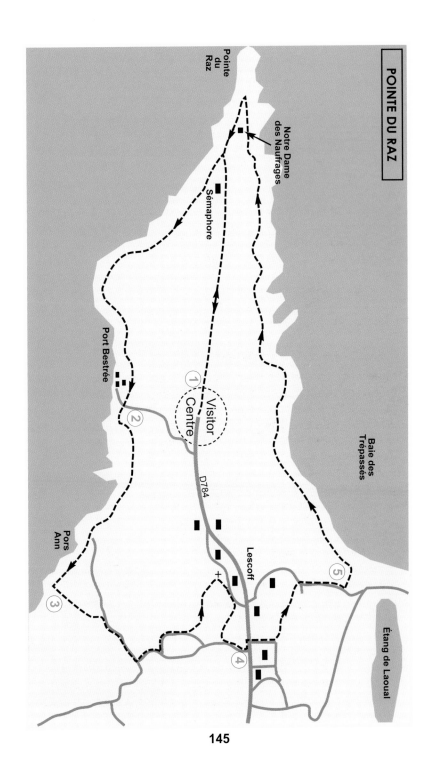

POINTE DU RAZ

Pointe
du
Raz

Notre Dame
des Naufrages

Sémaphore

Port Bestrée

Baie des
Trépassés

① Visitor
Centre

②

D784

Pors
Ann

③

Lescoff

④

⑤

Étang de Laoual

145

cove, Pors Ann, and then ascends the cliff once more. At its height, the yellow waymarks direct you to leave the GR and turn inland.

3. Now following the track across rough grassland, you reach a hard-surfaced road. Turn right and follow this to the village. At the road junction beside the first houses, turn left, uphill. Now take the first road on the left, which soon turns a sharp corner to the right. Ahead of you at this corner are two traditional low stone fishermen's cottages. After passing the calvary, take the first earth track on the left. This leads you downhill to an old lavoir on the stream at the bottom, and then climbs past the little stone Chapel of St-Michel. Here the path bears right between walls to arrive at a square with another calvary. Ahead of you is a very old stone house with carving around the tiny windows and doors. Turn right, and after 20m, at the junction, right again, still following the clear waymarking. Soon you are on a track between stone walls, and at its end, you bear left twice to reach the main road.

4. Cross the road to take a road on the other side, about 50m to the left, just before the Lescoff sign. This road brings you to a grassy area where a track leads down between houses on the left. The track soon corners and levels out along the top of a field. At the next track junction, bear right, and, coming to another lavoir, join the road to descend to the beautiful Baie des Trépassés - a curve of golden sand with the long Étang de Laoual behind it in the valley.

5. Before reaching the sandy bay, turn left, following the Sentier Côtier signs to a path running below the old blockhouses. This climbs with magnificent views of the bay as you go. The path is quite obvious - and at times quite precarious - as it clings to a cliffside. On rounding a headland and facing huge cliffs descending to the foaming sea, the path suddenly turns away. Very soon you are surprised to see the sémaphore and statue of Our Lady quite close at hand and you have no trouble following the path across the heather to reach the Point again.

**Notre Dame des Naufrages**

146

# More walks in the area

- There are also circuits including long sections of the coastal path along the south of the peninsula starting from Plogoff (16kms) and St-Tugen (13kms).
- You could follow the coastal path (GR34) as far as the Anse du Loc'h (just beyond Plogoff, approx. 10 kms) and return by bus, or, for something more ambitious, take the early bus from Audierne to the Pointe du Raz and return on foot - a distance of about 24kms along the most splendid shoreline.
- North of the Pointe du Raz, the coastal path skirts the Baie des Trépassés, then heads past the remote Chapel of St-They to the Pointe du Van which is much quieter than its neighbour. From here the views are magnificent - from Pointe de St-Mathieu near Brest, to the tip of the Crozon peninsula and across to the Île de Sein. Beyond the Pointe du Van, the coastal path then passes a succession of rocky viewpoints including an ornithological paradise (see below).

# Places of interest nearby

- Two boat companies make the one-hour crossing from Audierne to the Île de Sein. This is a low-lying treeless island, only 8.5 metres above sea level at its highest point. Twice in the 19th century it completely disappeared under the waves! It is now permanently inhabited by just a few fishing folk - although there is a village with two shops and a few restaurants for visitors. Long ago, the islanders made their living by plundering wrecks on the low reefs around its shores, but wrongdoings of the past were forgotten in the last war, when every able-bodied man on the island set sail for Britain to join the Free French Forces. For this, and for the part it played in the escape of thousands more, the island was awarded the Liberation Cross.
- The bird reserve at Goulien is open to visitors from mid-March to the end of August - the nesting season! Wandering along the paths on a cliffside scattered with wild flowers, you can observe cormorants, guillemots and a variety of gulls at their nesting sites.
- At Douarnenez there is a remarkable museum in the old harbour of Port-Rhu. Here 20 boats of all kinds are open for exploration - steam and sail craft, fishing boats and even a lightship are moored here. Back on dry land, a further 60 or more vessels are to be seen in the Musée du Bateau where they are worked on by traditional craftsmen.

## WALK 27 - Wildfowl on the river at LOCTUDY

| Length 11kms | Time 3hrs | Level Easy |
| --- | --- | --- |

**Location & parking:** Place de la Mairie, Loctudy. From Pont l'Abbé, follow the D2 south to Loctudy. Keep to the coast road, and the large car park is on your right, just before the port.

**Refreshments:** bars / restaurants in Loctudy, but none on route.

**Notes:** trainers adequate in dry summer weather, but sunken roads on the return can be muddy after rain. Some shade but take water with you, and binoculars to look at the wildfowl. (Map: IGN Top 25  0519 OT)

## Introduction

The wide calm tidal Rivière de Pont l'Abbé is at the heart of the Pays Bigouden - the south western corner of Brittany, named after the very tall hat of white lace, still worn by local women on festive occasions. This is a land steeped in tradition, its economy long based on the fishing industry. Loctudy is one of the main ports, and makes an exciting visit when the catch arrives in the early evening.

From the port at Loctudy you can look across the mouth of the Pont l'Abbé river to the little village of Île Tudy, just a few minutes ferry ride away on the far side. The journey by land will take a lot longer. Behind Loctudy, the river opens up into a wide flat expanse of tidal water with many creeks and inlets. This is a ria, a river valley flooded when sea levels rose many thousands of years ago - the river can still be seen flowing through the swamp at low tide. The vast mudflats continuously washed by briny waters and bordered by typical salt-loving vegetation are a paradise for the birds - herons, egrets, spoonbills, avocets, plovers, curlews, redshanks, shelducks and many others can be seen on the marsh. Winter is perhaps the best time for viewing them, when the river is also renowned for its large flocks of pintails.

If you have the opportunity, walk the length of the western shore of this river from Pont l'Abbé to Loctudy. In high season, a boat leaves Loctudy in the late afternoon and will return you to Pont l'Abbé in style. But since this is only possible in the summer months, and even then not every day, the walk described here is a circular one and includes the very prettiest stretch where pines and deciduous woodland reach to the river bank. The views change with the tide - the wide expanse of water at high tide reduces to only that of the original river bed at low. The shores become green and brown with coloured algae and a whole new plant life is revealed at the edge of the mud. At one point you reach a tide-mill, and a little further along, a menhir mouillé - a standing stone out in the water. Six thousand years ago, the river bank  was about at the level of the present low tide. Now the great menhir stands half-submerged at high water, and fully exposed only at low. A long crumbling jetty gives you a last look at the swollen river before you leave to return inland. On the way you can visit the eco-museum, a restored old farm at Kervaségan, before taking to the shady sunken lanes that return you to Loctudy.

## Directions

1. From the car park, cross the main road towards the sea, and turn left. Look for the GR waymarks and follow them (left) along the length of the river. At the roundabout, turn right following a sign to Circuit de Laë ar Barez. The road passes behind some big houses fronting the water and then descends to the dam across an entrant river. The track climbs on the far side of the dam.

2. Soon a junction is reached. (Here you have the option of turning right to take a tour of the headland of Penn ar Veur with its fine views of the river. The path is GR waymarked and will return you to this same point.) Continue along the road, and bear right in front of the entrance to the Château du Dourdy. The road now skirts a holiday village and arrives at the coast at the bridge to the Île Garo (private). Turn left here, following signs to Queffen. The path follows the edge of the bay through the attractive grounds of the château. Ahead you can see the little pine-clad island of Queffen, a bird sanctuary. Shortly you cross another dam, this time with a tide-mill. Keep ahead beside the river and then bear right to reach a tarmac road.

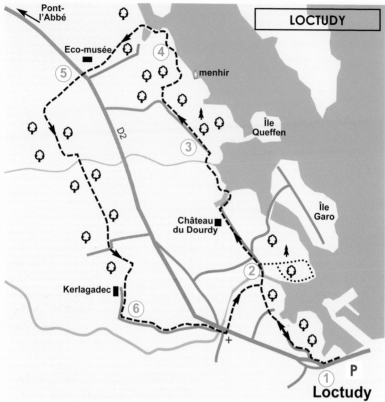

Loctudy

**3**. Turn left on the road, still following GR waymarks. Where the road takes a sharp left corner, keep straight ahead into the woods. A signpost indicates that this is the Site Naturel Protégé de Rosquerno. A little farther along, at the track junction, ignore sign ahead to Rosquerno, but turn right following orange marks towards the coast. At a clearing, the path turns sharply left, but to see the menhir bear right here. A signpost directs you to the Observatoire. Emerging from the oaks and pines you have a lovely view. Just off-shore stands the menhir, bands of colour around its thick body marking the extremes of tide, while across the calm waters lies the Île Chevalier. Turning away from the tranquil scene, return to the clearing and turn right following the GR waymarks. The path continues through the woods beside the river with views over the old jetty ahead.

**4**. Coming to a T-junction of tracks, ignoring the orange route left, turn right, still following the GR. This brings you down to the riverside at the end of the jetty - a fine viewpoint over the river.

**Menhir 'mouillé' at high tide**

From here turn left along the river and continue over the dam.
Immediately on the far side of this, take the first track on the left
and then bear right. This winds uphill through the woods
(occasional orange waymarks). After a bend to the left, turn
right at a T-junction, again uphill. Continue ahead beside fields
to finally emerge in the car park of the Eco-musée de Bigouden,
the Ferme de Kervaségan. Walk through the car park to the
main road.

5. Cross the road and take a wide track opposite, a few metres to
the right. This leads straight into the woods again, soon bearing
left and becoming a sunken track between banks (waymarked
orange). The track continues ahead for over a kilometre, broken
only by a bend to the left and then to the right near the Manoir
de Pen ar Prat. Eventually a tarmac road is reached, but very
soon this bears right, and once again you plunge into the woods
on a rough track. After 600m or so you reach the splendid
flower-bedecked old farm of Kerlagadec, and with it, more hard-
surfaced road.

6. This road soon takes a sharp left bend. Ignoring orange
waymarks on a track on the right, keep on the road for a further
800m, to where it joins the main road at a roundabout. Cross
over to the Chapelle de Croaziou to the right and then cross the
D2 directly to a broad track opposite, flanked by pine trees. This
avenue leads to the manor of Briemen, one of the riverside
houses you passed earlier, hidden behind a high wall. When
you reach it, turn right and retrace your steps to the car park at
Loctudy.

# More walks in the area

- If you are keen to walk all around the Rivière de Pont l'Abbé, the full circuit with the short ferry crossing, is 21kms.
- Two short walks (5-6kms) to be recommended are one including the Botanical Gardens at Raphalen and another in the south near Guilvinec where there are dolmens, an old chapel and three fountains, all within a few kilometres.
- Bigouden has a varied coastline - to the west are wide sands and dunes, the point of Penmarc'h (literally 'Horse's Head') is rocky, while the southern shores are prettier with creeks and fishing ports. The GR34 follows it all the way, and if you enjoy linear walks there are lots of possibilities.

# Places of interest nearby

- From Loctudy you can cruise to Bénodet and up the picturesque Odet River to Quimper. The trip from Loctudy to Pont l'Abbé (the return described in the text) is provided by the company Vedettes Bigoudènes.
- You can also take a trip to the Glénan Islands, about 10 miles out to sea. The largest island, St-Nicholas, will only take you about half an hour to walk around, but the islands again are a bird-watchers paradise!
- Just north of Loctudy is the Manoir de Kérazan. The rooms of this rambling stone manor have been restored to give an idea of life in its heyday in the 19th century.
- A little farther up the same road (D2) is the eco-museum that you passed on your walk. The Maison du Pays Bigouden is simply an old farmhouse, with outbuildings, tools and utensils, such as might have been found here a century ago.
- Further along the coast, the port of le Guilvinec presents its fishing industry at Haliotika,a discovery centre. High technology gives an insight into a life of battling with winds and waves on the high seas - try embarking on a virtual trawler!
- At the south-west tip of Bigouden is Penmarc'h, curiously dominated by the huge bulk of the Eckmuhl lighthouse - all 65m of it rising from a street near the sea front. The views from the top are magnificent - from the Île de Sein to Concarneau and out to the Glénan Islands. Just to the north is the rocky Pointe de la Torche, and some beautiful - if treacherous - beaches where windsurfers of amazing agility can be seen cavorting elegantly above the towering waves. Near one of these beaches is an excellent museum of pre-history.

## WALK 28 - MÉNEZ-HOM - a hill with a view!

| **Length** 13kms | **Time** 4hrs | **Level** Moderate |
|---|---|---|

**Location & parking:** church of Sainte-Marie du Ménez-Hom at the junction of the D887 (Châteaulin - Crozon) and the D47 from the direction of Douarnenez. Parking area opposite the church.

**Refreshments:** none at all on route. Take your own picnic – there is a picnic table beside the fontaine of the Chapelle Neuve.

**Notes:** gentle but sustained climb to the summit of Ménez-Hom. The track is a little rough - walking boots out of season or in wet weather. Carry water with you, take binoculars for the view from the top - and an abacus for counting all those spires!
(Map: IGN top 25 0518 OT)

## Introduction

Ménez-Hom looks out over the Bay of Douarnenez and all the ragged west coast of Brittany - and from its summit, 50 church spires can be seen. You could drive up here, but there is so much more to enjoy from the footpath! When you have admired the view, this walk takes you into a pretty valley with a sacred fountain.

Ménez-Hom is the last westerly outpost of the Montagnes Noires, almost an afterthought in the long ridge of granite hills. A mere 330m in height, its lack of altitude is more than compensated for by its superb location! To the west, it looks out over the bright blue Bay of Douarnenez encircled by the green arms of Cap Sizun and the Crozon peninsula, whilst farther north, the roadstead of Brest leads out to the Pointe de St-Mathieu. There is also a view of the estuary of the Aulne with the suspension bridge at Térénez and far away behind you are the Montagnes Noires and the Monts d'Arrée. On a clear day, the chapel of St-Michel can be seen over 15 miles away on top of Ménez-Mikel, the highest point in Brittany.

Of course, a place like this has its legend. On the north-west flank of the hill is a cairn said to be the burial place of King Marc'h, the wronged lover in the Tristan and Isolde saga. After their deaths, King Marc'h became a tyrannical ruler - although he did establish the church of Ste-Marie on the slopes below Ménez-Hom. It is said that his soul will be released to heaven when the cairn becomes high enough to afford a view of that church from its summit. Walking up this hill you may even meet the fair lady who invites wanderers to add a stone to the pile!

When at last you come down from Ménez-Hom, this walk takes you through a green valley where the fontaine has very special powers. Many of the remote churches in Brittany have a nearby fontaine (spring), the waters of which have specific powers of healing attributed to them. In this valley, the fontaine of the Chapelle Neuve is the place to bring an infant who is late in walking. First the child should be bathed in the waters and then sat on the little stone seat beside the well. Mother should then sit at the base of the nearby cross and call the infant - whereupon, he will get up and toddle over to her! The fontaine is in a pretty wooded site in the valley and there is a picnic table not far away.

The way home is up hill and down dale, through ancient farming hamlets and past a dolmen with a view over the bay. And when you return to Ste-Marie du Ménez-Hom, don't forget to look at the chapel itself - a 16th century version of the one founded by King Marc'h. It is notable for its ornate calvary and triumphal arch - and for its balustraded bell tower, which took over a century to complete.

## Directions

1. From the car park opposite the church, cross the main road and take the D47, direction Trégarvan. Take the left fork in about 1km, direction Kergaoc. A further 200m along this road, turn left on a yellow waymarked track leading into the woods. This leads steadily uphill through the pines. Look out for a sharp left-hand turn uphill at one point - but again the path is waymarked on a tree just past the junction. The pines thin as you go, and soon you climb to gorse-clad moorland above them. At length a GR joins you from the right and you turn left to follow its waymarks to the summit. The views open up as you go and you can see to the right the estuary of the Aulne with its suspension bridge. Soon you reach the borne - the concrete marker - on the summit. This peak is known in Breton as 'le Yed' and from here the views are best, rather than the orientation table farther on.

2. Just past the orientation table, walk down the steps and turn right, following yellow waymarks and those of the GR. This is a splendid descent through the gorse with fine views over the

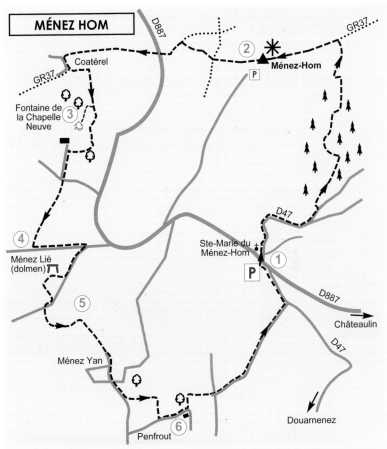

coast. There are often a few para-gliders on these slopes to
provide added entertainment. At the track-crossing half-way
down the slope, take the track opposite, and continue down to a
track T-junction near the road. Turn left to reach the road and
cross directly over to a yellow waymarked broad track opposite.
On reaching the pretty village of Coatérel, take the first road on
the left, and at the next junction, where the GR turns right,
continue straight ahead. This wide track bears left then right to
climb again, and about 500m from the village, a wooden
signpost directs you right to find the Fontaine de la Chapelle
Neuve. You probably won't have a crawling infant with you, but
the site is very picturesque and well worth a visit.

3. Retrace your steps to the main track. Now continue uphill
following yellow waymarks to a tarmac road leading to a farm.

Turn left here and continue to another tarmac road. Cross directly to a pleasant track lined by pines. After 300m there is a little clearing with a rustic seat and picnic table. Continue (with fine views over the bay on the right) to another road.

4. Turn left on this road (ignore yellow waymark on the track ahead). You can see traffic on the main road at the top of the hill, but about 200m before reaching it, double back on a road on the right. As you walk downhill again, you can see a dolmen in the field on the right. Reaching two trees beside the road, take the narrow track along the edge of the field to reach the Dolmen du Ménez Lié. From here the intended route continues to pass through the hedge on the left just beyond the dolmen and then follows along another hedge to reach the road again. If this route is overgrown, return the way you came. However you reached the road, turn right along it and as it corners right, look out for a broad track on the left. Take this downhill into the woods and then bear left to climb again.

**Dolmen du Ménez Lié**

5. At the cross-tracks, turn right on a broad track. At first through gorse and then through pines and chestnuts the path descends to the hamlet of Ménez-Yan. At the fork at the end of the houses, keep straight ahead, and about 200m farther on, as the road bends right, take a broad grassy track on the left. After a sharp right hand corner, this descends to the farm at Penfrout.

6. At the bottom of the hill, do not go into the farm, but turn left on the road. Just past a stone house, where the road turns sharply right, take a track on the left and again climb into the woods. This track soon corners right and continues to a cross-roads where you take the narrow road opposite. The road now climbs quite steeply for about a kilometre - the compensation is the increasingly fine view on the right. When you finally reach the road at the top, Ste-Marie du Ménez-Hom lies to the left and it will take you only another five minutes to reach the car-park opposite the church.

# More walks in the area

- If you are keen to visit more chapels with their healing fountains, there are several nearby circuits that will interest you. Starting from Lestrévet on the coast south-west of Ménez-Hom, there is a 10km route entitled the Circuit des Chapelles. This passes the famous chapels of St-Suliau and St-Côme, each of which has a spring said to have medicinal properties.

- St-Gildas, to the south-east of Ménez-Hom, has a chapel and fountain and is the starting point for another circuit of 9kms.

- Further east, near Châteaulin, is the Fontaine de St-Laurent, passed on an interesting circuit which also includes a long stretch along the banks of the Aulne with two locks. Further down the same river, yet another circuit starts from the Fontaine de St-Exuper.

- Another route worth a mention is that starting from Trégarvan on the estuary of the Aulne. Trégarvan is a very pretty village and probably worth visiting in its own right, but the circuit of 12kms also skirts the Aulne and climbs to the moorland and forest on the slopes of Ménez-Hom.

- There are also walking trails in the nearby Bois de Nevet, beautiful woods of beech, oak and chestnut. St-Ronan himself lived in these woods in the 6th century, and it was from here that he set out on his walks, fasting and barefoot - every 6 days he took the 12km circuit, and on the days in between, a short 5km climb up the hill.

# Places of interest nearby

- About 10kms east of Ste-Marie du Ménez-Hom is Châteaulin, a picturesque old town on a long loop of the River Aulne, which here is the start of the Nantes-Brest Canal. You can wander beside the quays and along the towpath and watch boats passing through the locks.

- The pretty town of Locronan with its well-preserved ancient houses, is just 10kms south of Ste-Marie du Ménez-Hom. Every six years, on the second weekend in July, Locronan becomes the scene of an extravagant Christian pilgrimage (the Grande Troménie) whose origins are druidic, but whose route of about 12kms follows in the steps of St-Ronan, Locronan's founding saint from Ireland. A Petite Troménie is held on each of the five interim years.

# A few words in Breton . . .

(spelling may vary according to local custom)

Aber . . . . . . . . . . . . . . . . . . . . . . . . . . . . . . . . . .estuary
Aven . . . . . . . . . . . . . . . . . . . . . . . . . . . . . . . . . . . .river
Beg . . . . . . . . . . . . . . . . . . . . . . . . . . .point or summit
Bihan . . . . . . . . . . . . . . . . . . . . . . . . . . . . . . . . . . .small
Bras . . . . . . . . . . . . . . . . . . . . . . . . . . . . . . . . . . . . .big
Breizh . . . . . . . . . . . . . . . . . . . . . . . . . . . . . . .Brittany
C'hi . . . . . . . . . . . . . . . . . . . . . . . . . . . . . . . . . . . . .dog
Du . . . . . . . . . . . . . . . . . . . . . . . . . . . . . . . . . . . . .black
Enez . . . . . . . . . . . . . . . . . . . . . . . . . . . . . . . . . .island
Fest-noz . . . . . . . . . . . . . . . . . . . . . . . . . .night festival
Groaz . . . . . . . . . . . . . . . . . . . . . . . . . . . . . . . . . .cross
Gwenn . . . . . . . . . . . . . . . . . . . . . . . . . . . . . . . . .white
Gwin . . . . . . . . . . . . . . . . . . . . . . . . . . . . . . . . . . .wine
Kastel . . . . . . . . . . . . . . . . . . . . . . . . . . . . . . . . .castle
Ker . . . . . . . . . . . . . . . . . . . . . . . .town, village, hamlet
Lan . . . . . . . . . . . . . . . . . . . . . . . .monastery, hermitage
Lann . . . . . . . . . . . . . . . . . . . . . . . . . . . . . . . . . .heath
Loc . . . . . . . . . . . . . . . . . . . . . .remote place, hermitage
Loc'h . . . . . . . . . . . . . . . . . . . . . .lagoon, coastal lake
Men . . . . . . . . . . . . . . . . . . . . . . . . . . . . .stone, rock
Menez . . . . . . . . . . . . . . . . . . . . . . . . . . . . . .mountain
Meur . . . . . . . . . . . . . . . . . . . . . . . . . . .large, important
Mor . . . . . . . . . . . . . . . . . . . . . . . . . . . . . . . . . . . .sea
Nevez . . . . . . . . . . . . . . . . . . . . . . . . . . . . . . . . . .new
Palud . . . . . . . . . . . . . . . . . . . . . . . . . . . . . . . . .marsh
Penn . . . . . . . . . . . . . . . . . . . . . . .head, end, summit
Plou . . . . . . . . . . . . . . . . . . . . . . . . . . . . . . . . .parish
Pors . . . . . . . . . . . . . . . . . . . . . . . . . . . . . . . . . . .port
Roc'h . . . . . . . . . . . . . . . . . . . . . . . . . . .rock, crag
Ruz . . . . . . . . . . . . . . . . . . . . . . . . . . . . . . . . . . . .red
Ti / ty . . . . . . . . . . . . . . . . . . . . . . . . . . . . . . . . .house
Unan, daou, tri, pevar, pemp . . . . .one, two, three, four, five

# And phrases to use yourselves . . .

Cheers / Good Health! . . . . . . . . . . . . . . . . . . .Yec'hed mat!
Thank you . . . . . . . . . . . . . . . . . . . . . . . . . . . . .Trugarez
Goodbye . . . . . . . . . . . . . . . . . . . . . . . . . . . . . .Kenavo
Good morning / afternoon . . . . . . . . . . . . . . . . . . .Demat
Good night . . . . . . . . . . . . . . . . . . . . . . . . . . . .Noz vat

# Useful French Walking Words

anse . . . . . . .a cove, a small bay
atteindre . . . . . . . . . . . .to reach
balisage . . . . . . . . .waymarking
bifurquer . . . . . . . . . . . . .to fork
blanc(he) . . . . . . . . . . . . .white
bleu(e) . . . . . . . . . . . . . . . .blue
bois . . . . . . . . . . . . . . . .a wood
bosquet . . . .a spinney, a copse
bourg . . . . . . . . . . . . . . .village
chemin . . . . . . . .a way, a path
colline . . . . . . . . . . . . . . .a hill
contourner . .to go round, to skirt
creux . . .sunken or hollowed out
dessous . . . . . . . . . . . . . .under
dessus . . . . . . . . . . . . . .above
droit (tout droit) . .straight ahead
droite . . . . . . . . . . . . . . . .right
église . . . . . . . . . . . . . .church
empierré . . . . .stony or metalled
emprunter . . . .to take (direction)
étang . . . . . .a small lake, a pool
en face . . . . . . . . . . . .opposite
fourche . . . . . . . . . . . . . .a fork
franchir . . . . . .to clear, to cross
gauche . . . . . . . . . . . . . . .left

goudronnée . . . . . . .tarmacked
grimper . . . . . . . . . . . . .to climb
hameau . . . . . . . . . . . . .hamlet
jaune . . . . . . . . . . . . . . .yellow
jusqu'à . . . . . . . . . . . .as far as
longer . . . .to go along, to follow
mare . . . . . . . . .a pond, a pool
mener . . . . . . . . . . . . . .to lead
monter . . . . . . . . . . . . .to climb
niveau . . . . . . . . . . . . .a level
patte d'oie . . . . .multiple junction
pente . . . . . . . . . . . . . . . .slope
prairie . . . . . . . . . . . .a meadow
rouge . . . . . . . . . . . . . . . . .red
route . . . .a road, track, direction
ruisseau . . . . . . . . . . . .a stream
sentier . . . . . .a footpath, a track
sous-bois . . . . . . . .undergrowth
suivre . . . . . . . . . . . . .to follow
talus . . . . . . . . . .a slope or bank
tourner . . . . . . . . . . . . . .to turn
traverser . . . . . . . . . . .to cross
variante . . . . . . .alternative route
vert(e) . . . . . . . . . . . . . .green
virer . . . . . . . . . .to bend or turn

**Rock carvings at Rothéneuf, Ille et Vilaine.**

159

# Other Red Dog guides

## FINISTERE
## Things to see and do at
## the End of the World
### by Wendy Mewes

14 separate tours by car, with maps, directions and suggestions for places to visit and landscape to explore in the most distinctively varied department of Brittany

£8.99  or  13.50 €

## WALKING
## and other activities in
## FINISTERE
### by Wendy Mewes

36 circular walks with maps and directions, and suggestions for 45 more. Also included is key information for other outdoor activities - golf, riding, water-sports, fishing and cycling

£8.99  or  13.50 €

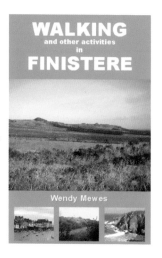

## These can be ordered through our website
### www.reddogbooks.com

160